GRAND JURY
AWAKE:

TACTICAL CIVICS™ Field Handbook
Volume 2

Grand Jury
Awake

TACTICAL CIVICS™ Field Handbook
Volume 2

DAVID M. ZUNIGA
Founder, TACTICAL CIVICS™

Other Books by David M. Zuniga

This Bloodless Liberty

Fear The People (4th Ed.)

Our First Right

A Tax Honesty Primer

A Republic to Save: Essays in Tactical Civics

Book One- *Tactical Civics*™

Book Two- *Mission to America: A 7-Week Crash Course
in TACTICAL CIVICS*™

The TACTICAL CIVICS™ *Ready Constitution*

Books in Progress

Book Three- *Engine of Change*

Book Four- *The Banished Bureaucrat*

Book Five- *The Greatest Awakening*

*The Statesman's Manual: A Citizen-Statesman's Guide to Writing and
Enacting Legislation Conforming to the Constitution and
Supporting the Rule of Law*

Dedication

This booklet is dedicated to every American who decides to begin
living as the Founding Fathers intended – to faithfully and
courageously perform every American's duties, and
give hope to those in other lands as we arrest DC
and state palace organized crime, ratchet back
the Deep State, and inspire our
unborn descendants.

CONTENTS

PREFACE

(Please don't skip this; it's bedrock.)

In America, you really are who you think you are.

Before you begin learning about one of the best kept secrets in our blessed Republic, I need to frame this little booklet – this study of civics, if you will – with some key concepts that prove why our civilization is so special. To many, it appears that we're about to lose it forever.

Being a Christian, I have a different take on the hijacking; if you've read my books, you know my position: we're *definitely* under God's judgment for refusing to glorify Him and for chasing after self, stuff, and sin. And the worst is yet to come, alas. From the Bible, we know that God always chastises those whom He loves. We also know that He's always faithful to restore us when we repent. It's a formula that we see God threading through His Word from Genesis to Revelation.

I believe that AmericaAgain! Trust and TACTICAL CIVICS™ are just a collection of normal, everyday Americans whom God is inspiring to stand up, crawl out of the shadows of faithless gloom, wash ourselves in His Word, and repent our faithlessness and abdication by doing the chores. As our HQ team knows, I always reiterate, "repentance is an action word", and I always speak about doing the chores because I grew up on a South Texas ranch where we raised everything from poultry to hogs and beef cattle.

In town or in the country, all of us have chores just by virtue of being blessed to be born in this Republic. In Volume 1 of this Handbook, our co-founder Matt Mida explains step by step how to start and lead a TACTICAL CIVICS™ county chapter. In this Volume 2, we explore our duty for Grand Jury; then in Volume 3, co-founder John Leyzorek explains our duty and authority for Militia and how to go from total ignorance to a restored, lawful Militia in every county. Just doing the chores. *No other people on earth have this authority, or this duty.*

So. Let's first dispel some preconceptions about Grand Jury, and about our system of justice…and…well, about *you*. Where you think you fit into America's rule of law. I'm willing to bet that even if you're a college

1

graduate, you've never faced this question before. So here I ask you to face it, think about it, and answer it in your own mind. Otherwise, this Handbook will be wasted effort.

As you'll soon read, our system of law is unique on earth now, and it is predicated on two ancient institutions *of the People* for *enforcing* law. When even a significant remnant of the People decide to shirk their chores, mankind's sin nature takes the controls and things get very bad.

We're there, right now. So…what does Grand Jury have to do with it?

If you are a natural-born or lawfully naturalized American, then no matter what your income or education level, or the color of your skin: *you have both the authority and the duty to serve Grand Jury and Militia duty in some capacity, on a regular basis.* Even those who very quickly use the excuse, "I'm too old", are very often just skipping out on chores, not realizing that 'Militia duty' can include support functions, some of them easily performed from a home computer in just a few hours per week.

Grand Jury duty is even simpler. Most Americans who want to serve, must be *allowed* to serve. You will learn in this handbook that the legal industry has attempted to shut down the Grand Jury in America as lawyers, judges, and bureaucrats have done in every other country on earth. It's *our choice* whether We The People allow that to happen.

Grand Jury is not like those dramatic nail-biter law movies. You're not in a trial; just overseeing your county. As a panel member of an inquest, *you* don't go out to collect evidence or verify important facts made by witnesses. Your Grand Jury Panel sends the prosecutor's staff member, or staff of the sheriff's office, or if the case is against court or paid law enforcement staffers, you'll need your county's Militia unit to execute your search warrants or subpoenas.

As a member of the Grand Jury, you must always remain unknown to the public and especially to the subjects of your inquests. One of the most vital duties of law enforcement in your county (including Militia, the Constitution's original volunteer law enforcement) is keeping Grand Jury members safe and hidden from the public. Demand it!

After your service on Grand Jury each time, you melt right back into the public. You do not tell others about your cases; a basic rule that keeps you safe, and keeps society functioning properly. While you are serving, *your Panel is the highest authority* in the county court system.

2

The Story in Your Head

Alasdair MacIntyre wrote, *I can only answer the question 'What am I to do?' if I can answer the prior question "Of what story do I find myself a part?* [1] A narrative is just a story. In Greek, μετα-(meta) means after, beyond, or behind; something comprehensive or transcending. So a *metanarrative* is an all-encompassing, grand story within which all other stories exist. Like a framework; not as big a framework as *worldview,* but a grand story. Unbelievers have a belief system in which naturalism and evolution are the metanarrative. The Bible presents the metanarrative that you and I believe, as did our Founding Fathers. Our culture was built on that metanarrative, and *it alone will save and restore our culture.*

What we tell ourselves about ourselves, even if all the facts aren't real (perhaps only ideals or wishes), we all conduct our lives based on our personal metanarrative. As I write this, the latest fad in metanarratives is a 50-year-old retread from drug-addled Hippies, called 'Critical Theory' or 'Social Justice', that Marxists teach their 'useful idiots' who consider themselves losers. So these young people lash out at 'winners'; the diligent, godly, successful, and contented. *Worse is coming.*

America's Four Unique Bulwarks

Besides Scripture, Americans have three more unique bulwarks that have built our systems of law, economics, government, and culture.

Some people choose the metanarrative of naturalism (everything is the result of random natural processes that began with ambitious slime), or of Hinduism (everything is an illusion created by an impersonal reality), or other religious frameworks. Others trust the Bible's metanarrative that everything is created by and for Jesus Christ. Your metanarrative will radically affect how you conduct and understand your life.

Look around the world; beliefs lead to profoundly different results. For instance, if you live in China, no matter how capitalism grows around you, you can't escape the fact that there are 1.4 billion other individuals, swarming to and from their huge apartment buildings and scurrying around on mass transit like insects, all of whom have been brought up in a 5,000-year-old culture of autocracy and conformity. As a Chinese citizen, you simply cannot believe or operate like an American, having

---

[1] Alasdair MacIntyre, *After Virtue: A Study in Moral Theory,* 2nd ed. (Notre Dame, IN: University of Notre Dame Press, 1984), 216.

actual power to pursue evildoers and take an active part in your legal system through Grand Jury and Militia. But that's not only unthinkable in China; it's unthinkable in England, Canada, Norway, and *everywhere else on earth*. America is blessedly unique via four bulwarks built over centuries: 1) The gospel of Jesus Christ; 2) The U.S. Constitution; 3) Grand Jury; and 4) Militia; that's just We The People when we 'execute the Laws of the Union, suppress Insurrections, and repel Invasions'.[2]

No other people on earth will ever have these four unique bulwarks.

Dishonor Where it's Due

Before I brief you on your authority and duty when serving on Grand Jury: be careful what words you use, and the honor that you bestow with your punctuation and terms. That honor is *not* warranted today.

The former dean of Stanford Law School, Larry Kramer, in his 2004 book, *The People Themselves: Popular Constitutionalism and Judicial Review,* posits that We The People got in this mess by forgetting that *we,* not the supreme Court, are the last word on the U.S. Constitution's meaning.

Oh, and *never* trust anything written by a lawyer or spoken by a preacher or politician (including sheriffs and judges) until you take the measure of the person *by actions*, not words. These people are trained to deliver pretty words. Notice the pit we're in, despite all their passionate speeches and sermons? Sane people don't think highly of speechifying 'professionals'; we'll sooner trust a farmer, mechanic, grandmother, or truck driver.

In retraining Americans to perform the duties and exercise the authority that we've had for over 230 years *over* our Constitution and its creatures, TACTICAL CIVICS™ employs a new writing convention in all of our publications. We The People, the (collective) sovereign in this Republic, must learn to capitalize 'People' and never capitalize the label or office of our servants: mayor, commissioner, sheriff, senator, congressman, president, justice, governor…

And *especially* we don't capitalize *judge.* If any species of servant has shown utter contempt for the Constitution, it's the egotistical petty emperors in black frocks. Likewise, we refrain from starting a sentence with the words *federal* or *government,* because we refuse to capitalize them.

---

[2] U.S. Constitution, Article I, Section 8, Clause 15.

Oh, we're fully aware of the 'rules' of address and punctuation in which we were programmed in school, college, university, in those writers' grammar manuals, and by every level of our servants, media, and corporate America. But just because my arrogant jailers want me to keep pulling my own cell door shut, does not mean I'll do it. Showing honor to people who look down their noses to steal from you, lie to you, and despise us, *their employers,* deserves nothing but *dis*honor.

Up until now, too many cynically believe it's enough to crack politician jokes like, "How do you know when a politician is lying? When his lips are moving." But with our rule of law on the cliff's edge or perhaps already in free-fall over the cliff, this is no time for jokes or cynical resignation. It's time to return to our chores.

If Americans understood the extent of their power to arrest corruption when they serve on Grand Jury, the roster of Grand Jury volunteers would include half the population of each county. As you will see in a few pages, we have inherited an ancient and now totally unique system in which the People themselves are the final authority to stop the 'bad guys'. In this Republic, by the grace of God, We The People made ourselves the top of the pecking order; the only human power *above* the Constitution.

This little book will teach you what no law school will, because they are a major part of the problem all around us. But the wonderful thing is, truth can still be known, and...

Some days, the world just changes.

INTRODUCTION
This is a Job for Grand Jury!

Which is more destructive, ignorance or crime?

First the bad news. Last November, a criminal cabal overthrew our government after first setting up the steal using the largest fraud ever perpetrated: the Chinese Communist Party's weaponized bat virus. The D.C. Deep State, in alliance with Marxist governors from coast to coast, and with Big Tech and all major media, used China's bioterror attack for their own domestic terror plan. It was the most heinous crime in American history, and the first time that a massive number of American criminals actually allied themselves with a foreign enemy to overthrow a president, wreck America's economy, and gaslight gullible Americans.

As I write this, 'Resident' Biden, a senile pedophile, lifelong politician and the elderly head of an international crime family, is only one of Barack Hussein Obama's puppets. After eight years sowing race war and economic collapse, Hussein Obama is still the kingpin of American Communism. Also part of the criminal cartel are the 535 counterfeiters, financial frauds, extortionists, spouse abusers, hot check artists, business failures, shoplifters, and a few honest men called Congress.

Unfortunately, all those criminals were elected by the same population who was first fooled by the ludicrous 9/11 story, then by Russiagate, Shampeachment, hundreds of orchestrated street riots, and then the bat virus mega-fraud in which Donald Trump himself played ringmaster.

So. You see that *ignorance* is more destructive; it allows crime to go wild. American ignorance keeps criminals in business.

Half a Century of Evidence

Criminologist Donald Cressey, in his 1969 book, *Theft of The Nation,* described how organized crime had deep-captured D.C. and the state palaces and was using them as lackeys. Peter Schweizer has published countless books on Congress' crimes...*Extortion, Throw Them All Out, Architects of Ruin, Secret Empires,* and *Profiles in Corruption.* Thomas

7

DiLorenzo's *Organized Crime: The Unvarnished Truth About Government*, categorizes Congress' crimes, while Peter Dale Scott's *American War Machine*, and *Drugs, Oil & War, The American Deep State*, and dozens more books go into great detail. Countless whistleblower books from former CIA, FBI, IRS and DC staffers offer mountains of evidence of crimes being committed right now by legislators, presidents, governors, and mayors. Crime reigns in America.

We The People haven't arrested criminals because most Americans don't realize that we can, and in fact that it's our duty. We don't recognize the widespread crimes and *civil disobedience* being committed by our servants at every level. In his book *The City of God*, St Augustine explained that civil authority without justice is just a band of thieves: *"Justice being taken away, then, what are kingdoms but great robberies?"* [3]

But now the good news. We're living in *the best time in American history* and there's no statute of limitations on treason and overthrowing government by stealing an election. We can *enforce* the Constitution because as I said above, We The People are (collectively) the sovereign *over it,* as we clearly stipulate in the opening words of that Law.

By God's grace, TACTICAL CIVICS™ offers a repentant, responsible new way of life for Americans to begin enforcing the U.S. Constitution for the first time. This isn't politics; it's *law enforcement* via the People's two ancient institutions, the Grand Jury and Militia in each county.

American Communism Unmasked

The Biden overthrow is *surreal;* if not so pathetic, it would be funny to see such gullibility and passivity in the face of this Deep Axis *coup d'etat.* Because Big Tech and all major media are now 'state media' and co-conspirators just as in all Communist countries, the masses believe what they see and hear. Gaslighting projects throughout Trump's presidency illustrate the ruthless depths to which 'the system' will go to maintain its control of clueless, partying, consuming oxen. [4]

America's hijacked condition and criminality from school boards to Washington DC didn't begin 20 years ago with the 9/11 operation. A century of crimes planned and committed from the corrupt city-state

---

[3] Augustine, *The City of God;* Book III, Paragraph 28

[4] Communist China was part of it also; see *Unrestricted Warfare* (1999) by CCP military officers and party bureaucrats Qiao Liang and Wang Xiangsui. *They're here.*

on the Potomac transformed servant government into even more organized crime than the above authors list. Congress and governors are running fully *Communist* operations. They open the border to millions more illegal aliens to add to tens of millions here, to fatten industry bottom lines and put millions more Americans out of work, so they and the illegals all become government dependents.

A Real Solution at Last

Electing new politicians can't fix this. The election overthrow was the last straw, but the military could do nothing about the hijacking; the Posse Comitatus Act forbids it, and the military is shot through with truly un-American officers. Only Militia can lawfully arrest the crimes by ruthless public servants pushing Obama's dream. *Elections truly can't fix this.*

Over 12 years and 60,000 hours we developed TACTICAL CIVICS™, the only full-spectrum solution. We The People have the authority and lawful power to arrest corrupt actors and end the hijacking before it's too late. We need to build our numbers, then in every county, restore the Constitution's two law enforcement institutions. That's the purpose of our online Training Center. We *can* arrest the hijacking; but you must do your part. *And this restoration will demand time, grit, and commitment.*

Handbook Synopsis

You'll learn in Chapter 1 that the origins of Grand Jury and Militia are over 1,000 years old and have been attacked by lawyers for a century. In Chapter 2, you'll learn about our County Grand Jury Ordinance, why it's crucial, when and how to get it enacted, and the web pages that your county government must add to its website to allow citizens to learn about and also to volunteer for Grand Jury, and submit confidential information on potential criminal activity.

In Chapter 3, you'll learn how a Grand Jury is impaneled and how to handle corrupt judges. Chapter 4 explains the authority, independence, duties, and responsibilities of the Grand Jury. Chapter 5 discusses the oath that Grand Jury members take and why the institution must remain secret. In Chapter 6, you'll learn what to do when citizens call for a Grand Jury but are blocked by corrupt servants.

Chapter 7 explains the difference between a *presentment,* an *indictment,* and an *information,* the three documents and processes that initiate prosecution. Chapter 8 discusses the Grand Jury's major tools, the *subpoena* and *warrant*. In Chapter 9, we will introduce the most groundbreaking aspect of TACTICAL CIVICS™ – how the Grand Jury employs County Militia to execute subpoenas and warrants when paid 'law enforcement' is the target or is unwilling to support the Grand Jury. Finally, in Chapter 10 we discuss why Home Rule is vital to the fabric of our republic.

The Origin of Grand Jury's Authority

Far from taking the law in our own hands, you'll see here that *in Grand Jury, the law has been in the People's hands for over a thousand years!* First, remember that the rights of man come from God. Secondly, don't ask, "where does Grand Jury get its authority?" The proper question is, where does *government* get its authority?

Below is an infographic of American civics. Note that We The People *are the Boss* over government. The notes on the right margin are key: those who take an oath to obey, are government *servants*. We The People are government *sovereigns,* 'living above the line'.

10

Supreme Over the Supremacy Clause

After considering centuries of natural law, common law, civil law, and constitutions of every form of government, our Founding Fathers leapfrogged Aristotle, Cicero, and Aquinas; they stopped to admire Montesquieu, Burke, Hobbes, Paine, Locke, and Bolingbroke, but they wanted more liberty than monarchy could offer.

Yet, understandably proud at conquering the most powerful army and navy on earth, some American colonists wanted George Washington to be king. The popular general would have none of it, and the delegates to the Philadelphia convention had a far more exciting new form of government in mind. In some ways it was as revolutionary as the French Revolution that followed; but our forefathers learned from history, and unlike the French, they considered the Bible to be society's bedrock.

The written Constitution they spent four long months crafting together has inspired the world for over 230 years since. The oldest surviving written constitution in history, the first three words fired the most stunning shot; the most unique phrase in the history of constitutions:

We The People.

The phrase was not artistic flourish. As the first chief justice John Jay wrote in the first major U.S. supreme Court opinion,

> *The People are Sovereign...at the Revolution, the sovereignty devolved on the People...the citizens of America are equal as fellow citizens, and as joint tenants in the sovereignty.*[5]

In his own concurring opinion, justice James Wilson agreed, and Wilson was a true authority. The Scots-American statesman, legal scholar, and Founding Father was twice elected to the Continental Congress, was a signer of our Declaration of Independence, a major drafter of our Constitution, and among the six original justices appointed by George Washington to the supreme Court. The first Professor of Law at the University of Pennsylvania, he taught the first course on the new Constitution...to George Washington and his cabinet! Wilson held that the People themselves are the collective sovereign of this Republic and there's no higher office in our government. Americans considered the matter settled; but over time, our servants became our masters.

---

[5] Chisholm v. Georgia, US 2 Dall 419, 454 (1793)

Back to our page 10 infographic; let me explain the tiny note under 'state courts'. We've always been taught that the Supremacy Clause means that whatever federal government does, it's the boss and that's that; shut up and dig, citizen! But that's nonsense; the Supremacy Clause is Article VI, Section 2 of the Constitution, and it reads:

> *This Constitution, and the <u>Laws of the United States which shall be made in Pursuance thereof</u>; and all Treaties made, or which shall be made, under the Authority of the United States, shall be the supreme Law of the Land; and <u>the Judges in every State shall be bound thereby,</u> any Thing in the Constitution or Laws of any State to the Contrary notwithstanding.*

The underlining is mine. As to the first underlined bit, concluding his opinion in the case of *Marbury v Madison*, U.S. supreme Court chief justice John Marshall wrote,

> *In declaring what shall be the supreme law of the land, the Constitution itself is first mentioned; and not the laws of the United States generally, but those only which shall be made in pursuance of the Constitution, have that rank.*

> *Thus, the particular phraseology of the Constitution of the United States confirms and strengthens the principle, supposed to be essential to all written constitutions, that a law repugnant to the Constitution is void; and that courts, as well as other departments, are bound by that instrument.*[6]

In other words, any federal law *not* in pursuance of the Constitution, or *repugnant* to the Constitution, is not only *not* the supreme law; it's void, meaning that it's no law at all. In Article I, we create Congress; in Article II we create the presidency. In Article III we create our high Court, and authorize our new creature Congress to create *inferior* federal courts; creatures of *our* creature, Congress. So what's supreme in the supremacy clause? *The Constitution!* And We The People are sovereign over *that*.

Now as to the second underlined phrase, and the page 10 infographic. Our state courts existed *before* the People created the Constitution. We bind state judges to *obey* the Constitution and to *enforce* it when required. We The People have always had superintendence over the snakes who pretended to represent us in DC, going there with modest net worth but retiring as multi-millionaires with fat pensions, even if we fired them for non-performance! *Face it: we've been fools.*

---

[6] *Marbury v. Madison,* 5 U.S. (1 Cranch) 137 (1803)

Of course, legislators are not our only rogue servants. So we must return to that thousand year old, tried and tested law enforcement tool used by populations even against kings. We The People mention juries in Article 3, Section 2 and in the Fifth, Sixth and Seventh Amendments. As we stipulate in the Seventh: *"No fact tried by a jury shall be otherwise re-examined in any Court of the United States."* When you're the target, a jury of your peers has the final say. It's critical to free people to inspect our servants' work for criminality while also being able to be judged by our peers, not by our servants.

We the People must not allow judges, prosecutors, court staffers, and sheriffs to operate unsupervised as they do today. In each county, the People must serve in Grand Jury and Militia to maintain law and order. As for Election Steal 2020: educated Grand Jury and restored Militia, working together in just a handful of counties can bring the criminals to justice, restoring our elections and rule of law.

As for re-seating the lawfully-elected Trump, there is no guidance in the Constitution as to who resolves a stolen election and a fraud junta in office, but since the People are sovereign, we can decide if we want the SCOTUS or Congress to do it.

If we hand down a sufficient number of indictments and supporting evidence to Congress, Trump will be quickly restored. Steve Bannon has an interesting proposal: since a Speaker of the House need not be a member of Congress, if the GOP wins the House back in 2022 they could install Trump as Speaker, then impeach 'resident Biden' and his criminal moll, and Trump would be next in line for president according to the Constitution. (Besides the fake Biden and Harris, a handful of fake congressmen and senators seated in January 2021 will also relinquish their seats to the actual winners.)

DC's five-year crime spree is massive; the emotional, business, financial, and societal damage is difficult to estimate yet. But we know that the junta includes the Democrat party, Chinese Communist Party with its bioweapon, and a staggering gaslighting campaign by DC organized crime, major media, Big Tech and others. Beginning with 'Russiagate', then Shampeachment of Trump and finally a stolen election via massive mail-in ballot fraud set up by a fake 'pandemic' terrorizing America. But actually, the gaslighting began with the 9/11 operation 20 years earlier.

America's 150-year hijacking has been God's judgment. We The People became godless and lazy. For generations, Americans were known for fearing and serving God; but in the 'enlightened' humanist generation of Lincoln, Marx, and Darwin, Americans increasingly feared and served evil men.

In the five generations since Lincoln's cannons fell silent, we've reaped the whirlwind, each successive generation more willing to banish and even defy God while allowing every form of evil and perversion into schools, the public square, so-called 'entertainment', clothing styles, 'music', and family mores. We have followed the way of England, away from God and toward self-destructive secularism. But of course…

Repentance is always an option.

CHAPTER 1
County Grand Jury: Origins, History, Enemies

A Grand Jury is the People's ancient legal body empowered to conduct official, secret inquests in the county court to investigate potential criminal conduct to determine whether a serious (felony) crime appears to have been committed or is being committed, and bring criminal charges so that a criminal case may proceed to court.

Grand Juries could have prevented Election Steal 2020. This book is one of only two histories about the Grand Jury, that was not written by lawyers[7]. We must reclaim this vital law enforcement institution that belongs to us and can only be performed by us.

Richard D. Younger's 1963 book, *The People's Panel: The Grand Jury in the United States, 1634-1941* is the action-packed history of how Americans stopped corrupt city, county, state, and federal government actors for three centuries, and how lawyers and judges in the state and federal systems have sought to kill the People's weapon against corruption. I found a copy years ago for under $20, but it's much more expensive now, so TACTICAL CIVICS™ is publishing a reprint of this vital work that must remain available to our descendants.

The history of Europe and the island monarchy of England is a long, confusing series of fights, claims, wars, assassinations, intrigues, and agreements between royal families and their high-born, landholding friends, and ever-shifting nests of popes and bishops. In ancient times, the Latin *Rex Lex* meant "the king is law". The powerful guy with the crown and troops could do anything he wanted, to anyone in his realm. He could take your stuff, your wife, your kids – *or you* – without asking, and for no reason. Rule of men has been the default position in history because the good guy always thinks, "Nobody can really be *that* bad, can they?" until the bad guys have his property, family, labor, and liberty. You see? That's our situation now, due to our ignorance.

---

[7] The other is Jason W. Hoyt's excellent book, *Consent of the Governed*.

On the other hand, *Lex Rex* means "the law is king"; our American system. *Rule of law* means that a code of norms is agreed to by all. The law rules; men don't. Author of one of the seminal works of western civilization, Henry de Bracton declared that the state is under God and the Law, *"because the law makes the king. For there is no king where will rules, rather than the law."*[8]

Our rule of law was not born in a Philadelphia meetinghouse in 1787, but with the Dooms of Ethelred (997, 1014 AD), then the rest of our Constitution's genealogy is the Charter of Liberties (1100 AD), Magna Carta (1215 AD), Provisions of Oxford (1258 AD), Declaration of Arbroath (1320 AD), Mayflower Compact (1620), Petition of Right (1628), Grand Remonstrance (1641), English Bill of Rights (1689), Declaration of Independence (1776) Articles of Confederation (1781) and finally, our Constitution – the culmination of an 800-year western rule of law. We The People are sovereign over it to defend it, and the Grand Jury and Militia are our weapons that we stipulate for the task.

The Timeless War for Law

Time out of mind, people have felt the pain of marauders stealing their land, homes, liberty, and future. In ancient times, they didn't wait for *the marauder himself* to tell them when and how they would be able to recover or retaliate. How silly would *that* be?

Tens of millions of Americans are seething in anger at having our republic stolen from us in a criminal election process, after Russiagate, Shampeachment, BLAntifa, and Chinavirus hoaxes. Yet notice that the whole time, people expected *federal* agencies to arrest *federal* criminals?

As for Election Steal, Americans think that they need to wait for state legislative tribunals to work like snails through the discovery process while the People sit and watch, because we are ignorant of civics! So now, go back to the infographic on Page 10, and *for the rest of your life, never forget that hierarchy.*

Our Constitution is the most magnificent law ever forged by mankind in the history of civilizations. Until you grasp its power, you will continue to cluck your tongue and scratch your head at criminals in city hall, the state palace, or in the DC city-state. This 3-volume series of

---

[8] Bracton, H., *On the Laws and Customs of England*, Vol. II, pg. 33 (1968).

Field Handbooks from TACTICAL CIVICS™ are the first weapons of their kind ever forged in history. Small but powerful by the counsel of the Holy Spirit, and from the memories brought out of the Old Dark of western civilization. This is a booklet of tactics and procedure. But first in this longest chapter, it's a brief lesson in our history. When we remember the lessons of history, we are not doomed to repeat them.

Imperium Romanum II

American authors compare America to the ancient Roman Empire, but that is inaccurate civics. The only empire in America that is chillingly similar to the ancient Roman Empire is Washington DC and its satellite courts and federal buildings across the sovereign States; an occupying power not only in exotic, faraway Hawaii and Alaska, or (as it claims) in Guam, Puerto Rico, the Marshall Islands, 'American' Samoa, the 'U.S. Virgin Islands', and so on, but Washington DC is also an *illegal occupying power* in all 48 contiguous states in this Republic.

By 'illegal occupying', I refer to the fact that 75% of present-day DC agencies, bureaus, departments, officers, and regulations are nowhere authorized by us in the Constitution. The DC Empire is a feral beast unauthorized in law and growing by the year. We've all sensed it; yet in a childishly irrational response we look to the beast to arrest itself! We have often explained in our books and podcasts: look up Marx's definition of Communism and Mussolini's definition of Fascism, and see that DC has been Communist and Fascist for over a century.

Our Feral Creature is Loose

Once again, flip back to the page 10 infographic of our government; see the first three words of that law by which We The People *create* a servant government in three branches? The People are the *creator,* and the three branches are our *creatures* – the things created by us through that law. We live and work *above the line;* and our servants, *below the line.*

The word *feral* refers to a formerly domestic animal that's gone wild. So the reason you've felt so disconcerted for years, as though we're suddenly living in a foreign land, is that the creature that we stipulate can only serve us in 17 specific functions, became feral. It coerces us with agencies, laws, and regulations that it made up out of thin air without our knowledge or consent.

Now it will increasingly demand our civilization, too. Will you fight it?

Thomas Jefferson said that we should bind our creature with "the chains of the Constitution", but he was inaccurate. The chains *in* the Constitution are the Grand Jury and Militia, and neither was forged by the Constitution; they existed in colonial America from the beginning, and for eight centuries prior to that, in England.

Now let's step back to see the birth of the People's amazing authority that now exists in America alone of all the legal systems on earth.

One of These Things is Not Like the Others

There are three general systems of law in the world: *common* law, *civil* law, and *canon* law. Like one-third of the countries on earth, our legal system comes from English Common Law, which originated in the early tribal law of the northern Germanic Angle and Saxon tribes in what is now Denmark, which law was called *volkriht* or later, 'folkright'.

As I explain the first of our 6-part podcast series, *Who Killed America's Militia?,* these same Germanic warrior tribes were also the embryonic form of the militia in England, thus of our own Militia.

Our system of law is very different from civil law (legislative orders and regulations) or canon law (religious orders and regulations) and is called *Common Law* later because it was common to all the king's courts across the island of England, but before that, because it was common to all the tribes of that island.

Civil Law systems are descended from Babylonian law via the Roman Empire. They are made by legislators, regulators, and bureaucrats who love enlarging their fiefdoms and personal power with rules, regulations, fees, and fines. European countries use civil law systems. The petty, blue-light tyrant nature of civil law is one reason that so many Europeans and others flee to America. We're 'the Land of the Free' due to our Common Law legal system, where the People are the top level of government. Or we *will* be, when we return to our chores.

When the ancient English kings began converting to Christianity, they no longer possessed the arbitrary power over the lives and families and property of the people. They could no longer randomly change the laws of their kingdom willy-nilly as they pleased. The monks and bishops taught England's kings about God's promise in Isaiah 10:1, to mete His judgment on civil authorities who enact unjust laws. Scripture has many

18

references to God's condemnation of those who pervert justice[9]. In explaining why the English people had so much more freedom than the French, Charles Spurgeon said,

> 'There is no land beneath the sun where there is an open Bible and a preached gospel, where a tyrant long can hold his place. It matters not who he be, whether pope or king; let the pulpit be used properly for the preaching of Christ crucified, let the Bible be opened to be read by all men, and no tyrant can long rule in peace. England owes her freedom to the Bible; and France will never possess liberty, lasting and well-established, till she comes to reverence the gospel, which too long she has rejected. There is joy to all mankind where Christ comes. The religion of Jesus makes men think, and to make men think is always dangerous to a despot's power…The man no longer cringes and bows down; he is no more willing, like a beast, to be led by the nose; but, learning to think for himself and becoming a man, he disdains the childish fears which once held him in slavery.'[10]

But never underestimate the power of a bureaucrat trying to fatten his career or add to his power over you. As a species, the worst offender in this category is judges; probably the second worst is state's attorneys. Now we begin a new era in American life, if God grants that a sufficient number of Americans will repent and begin fulfilling our duties over our Constitution. To do that, we must first lose the irrational fear of our servants, and the ridiculous idea that the FBI or DOJ, who are servants of our creature Congress, will somehow bring law and order.

Again return to our page 10 infographic. As we become responsible over the hired help, always remember that the most potentially crooked and tyrannical people are federal judges. Notice: We The People are at the *top* of that hierarchy and federal judges are at the *bottom!*

Sure, federal judges can call guns to their aid, screaming "Contempt of court!" but We The People will now begin restoring our Grand Jury and Militia in each county so we can finally arrest this widespread *Contempt of The People and of the Constitution!* Don't you think it's time for the Boss to wake up and start giving civics lessons to our servants in black frocks? You will, when you learn to serve on Grand Jury.

---

[9] See, for instance, Psalm 94, Proverbs 17:5 and 24:23, Exodus 23:7, Deuteronomy 16:18, Habakkuk 1:4, Isaiah 60:14, Lamentations 3:34

[10] Spurgeon, C.H., *'Joy Born at Bethlehem'*, Metropolitan Tabernacle Pulpit, 23 Dec 1871

A Republican Form of Government

So far as the Common Law principles relating to Grand Jury are in force in the various states, the law and decisions are predictable. In any state that has adopted a code of criminal procedure, the Common Law principles relating to Grand Jury are a vital part of that code, and court decisions will align with the Common Law.

But where the Common Law has been superseded by lawless statutes and 'regulatory' agencies with no basis in the Constitution, decisions conflict with the Common Law due to differences in the constitutions or statutes of the states. With Americans being so mobile now, citizens need to understand how vital rule of law is. If every time you move to another state, you're moving into a new morass of 'administrative law' (an oxymoron) then such states fail to maintain the constitutional republic[11] that we guarantee one another.

We The People, organizing lawfully and effectively county by county, is the objective of our projects called Grand Jury Awake™ and American Militia 2.0™ so today's clown show will not last. Behind the scenes, Obama may be smiling now, and corrupt judges can say what they like. But we vastly outnumber them, we have the Law on our side, and we're collectively sovereign over it. So *don't fear the servants.*

The Birth of Grand Jury

Many historians claim that it began after the Norman Conquest in 1066 A.D., and a Philadelphia lawyer named George J. Edwards published a book, *The Grand Jury,* in 1906 claiming that the institution may trace back even earlier than the dooms of King Ethelred. But since there are many claims on date of origin, we'll stake our claim, saying only that King Ethelred ordered the first *clearly published* call for a Grand Jury in his Doom of 997 AD, at Wantage:

> *There shall be an assembly in every hundred, and in that assembly shall go forth the twelve eldest knights and the reeve along with them, and let them swear...that they will never knowingly accuse an innocent man nor conceal a guilty man.*

---

[11] This is what we mean in Article IV, Section 4 of the Constitution where we stipulate that the United States will guarantee to every State, "a republican form of government".

20

As mentioned above, Volume 3 of this Field Handbook will introduce you to Militia, born in King Ethelred's Doom of 1014 AD (Ethelred was quite the innovator):

Let God's law be henceforth zealously loved by word and deed; then will God soon be merciful to this nation. ...Let landowners repair local defenses on every side, and bridges & armaments also be diligently attended to, according to what is always prescribed when there is need.

A *hundred* was a political subdivision of a *shire,* in ancient England. The word *shire* is from the Old English *scír* (official charge) and Old High German *scíra* ('care'). So, *shire* became synonymous with *county,* a term introduced to England in the Norman Conquest. A *reeve* was the tax collector and enforcer for the king and each shire had a *shire reeve,* which over time became shortened to *sheriff.*

Notice King Ethelred's Dooms are very free-market and capitalist? Government didn't do everything for the people or even royal subjects. Instead, the people were expected to provide their own homes, walls, bridges, and arms and keep them in good repair. To see why the heavy hand was impossible, we must reach back before Ethelred.

When the Visigoths attacked Rome in 406 A.D., Roman legions had occupied the island of England for 350 years. Like the U.S. Corps of Engineers across these 48 states, the legions had built highways and administrative posts for Roman bureaucrats to oversee. But now Rome had to pull her legions out of England to defend Rome, leaving England without those bossy bureaucrats and aristocrats, who fled to the Continent under Rome's protection, as the Anglo-Saxon folkways and folkright returned.

So when you read the Dooms of Ethelred, understand that for centuries before on that island, as J.R. Green wrote in his 1874 book, *A Short History of the English People,* among the Anglo-Saxons, "The man of noble blood enjoyed no legal privilege amongst his fellows".

But Does it Have Bluetooth?

But because historians argue so much amongst themselves about who did what back in the Old Dark centuries, we settle on 997 AD, with King Ethelred calling on the people to hold their own common law Grand Juries, and in his Doom of 1014, calling the people to arm themselves. So while Ethelred did give birth to people's Militia, it wasn't out of the kindness of his heart. Here's that back story, very briefly.

Sometime around 985 AD, a young Dane named Sweyn Forkbeard revolted against his dad, Harald Bluetooth. Sweyn took the throne of the Danes, drove his dad into exile, and in just over 25 years, had overthrown many jarls (Norse chieftain kings) and ruled all of Denmark and most of Norway. So he hopped over to England, as Vikings tended to do back then, and did to Ethelred what he had done to his Bluetooth dad. Ethelred fled into exile on the Continent with his sons, and Sweyn declared himself King of England on Christmas Day 1013.

And then he died, five weeks later. So the English nobles had a delegation go call Ethelred back to his old throne. But this time with conditions!

The Compact of Ethelred is found in the *Anglo Saxon Chronicle.* It's the first recorded pact between king and subjects in English history. To get his throne back, Ethelred had to declare his loyalty to the nobles, reform everything they disliked, and had to forgive all that had been said and done against him in his previous reign. From the Old English:

> *They [the counsellors] said that no lord was dearer to them than their natural lord, if he would govern them more justly than he did before. Then the king sent his son…with his messengers and bade them greet all his people and said that he would be a gracious lord to them, and reform all the things which they hated; and all the things which had been said and done against him should be forgiven on condition that they all unanimously turned to him without treachery. And complete friendship was then established with oath and pledge on both sides, and they pronounced every Danish king an exile from England forever.[12]*

As you complain about imperious judges and sheriffs, see what the English people did for us all those centuries ago. How can you complain about corruption yet not give a fig for Grand Jury?

It's Assize Too Small

Remember I said that some historians claim the Grand Jury was born after the Norman Invasion? Dick Helmholz held that the Grand Jury was born 169 years later than it actually was:

---

[12] Translated from the Old English *Anglo Saxon Chronicle*

The modern Grand Jury traces its origins to the Assize of Clarendon, an enactment of King Henry II in 1166. The Assize called for inquiry to be made, by the oath of twelve men from every hundred and four men from every vill, as to what persons were publicly suspected of robbery, murder, or theft or of receiving men guilty of those crimes. The crimes covered were expanded ten years later by the Assize of Northampton to include forgery and arson, and…grew to include almost all serious crimes. Under the procedure called for by the Assize of Clarendon, the suspected criminals were presented before royal justices, and then their guilt or innocence was determined by the judgment of God; that is, by ordeal. From this method of inquiry and presentment of persons suspected of serious crimes, later expanded…grew the two-stage process of indictment and trial that we recognize as the essence of common law criminal procedure.[13]

As I said, historians can't agree whether Ethelred, or Henry II (200 years after the Anglo-Saxon period) originated Grand Jury, and there are other claims made by legal historians. But the preponderance of evidence I've been able to dig up leads me to choose Ethelred's Doom of 997 AD at Wantage as the birth of Grand Jury and of western law in all Common Law countries.

The Johnny-Come-Lately Charter

Historian Patrick Wormald agrees; as he reported at the Millenary Conference celebrating a millennium since King Ethelred: *Though Aethelred's secular laws do not represent anything strikingly original, they help to explain, by their continuity with what went before and came after, the fact that the Anglo-Saxons presented their Norman conquerors with a system of centrally directed legal administration which is unparalleled in eleventh century Europe, and which is a vital reason, if not the vital reason, why England still has a system of native common law rather than one of Roman civil law.*[14]

It's too bad there's not a *Dooms of Ethelred Trust,* but there is a Magna Carta Trust that holds similar shindigs, to commemorate the charter of King John on June 15, 1215. John wanted to keep his crown and his head, but English barons had been overtaxed and over-plundered too

---

[13] R. Helmholz, *The Early History of the Grand Jury and the Canon Law* (50 U. of Chicago Law Review, pg 613)
[14] Patrick Wormald. *Æthelred the Lawmaker* in Hill, David (ed.), Ethelred the Unready: Papers from the Millenary Conference (1978).

long by him and his sheriffs; so with their private troops, they surrounded London and made John a deal he couldn't refuse.

These charters usually just stipulated that the People want control of their own lives, especially when brought up on trumped-up charges by zealous sheriffs. Ethelred, the inventor of Militia and Grand Jury gets the short end of historians' stick from W.S. McKechnie:

> *By the Assizes of Clarendon and Northampton, he established the principle that criminal trials should (in the normal case) begin with indictment of the accused by a representative body of neighbours sworn to speak the truth...The jury of accusation (or presentment), instituted in 1166, has continued in use ever since, passing by an unbroken development into the Grand Jury of the present day.*[15]

But Magna Carta expert Bruce O'Brien at the University of Mary Washington, claims that almost 150 agreements, pacts, and charters came before Magna Carta. In any case, ever since Ethelred in 997 AD, kings had to place themselves under the law, and they actually called on *the People themselves to rule* in legal matters in their hundreds, their shires, and their counties, over the law of the land and over the Common Law.

I will say one thing for Magna Carta; see its Section 61:

> *And we will seek to obtain nothing from anyone, in our own person or through someone else, whereby any of these grants or liberties may be... diminished, and if any such thing be obtained, let it be void and invalid...*

Note there the seed of our American legal principle that began with justice Marshall's opinion in *Marbury v. Madison* (1803) holding that any law that violates the U.S. Constitution is void; is no law at all.

Early America

During our War for Independence, British soldiers who were stationed here often found themselves the subject of Grand Jury *presentments* (see Chapter 7; a Grand Jury can receive or also issue a presentment). Grand Juries supported our American cause by writing presentments against those who joined the British army or who gave information to the enemy. They used Grand Juries as a propaganda tool in the months following publication of the Declaration of Independence. Rather than

---

[15] W.S. McKechnie, *Magna Carta: A Commentary on the Great Charter of King John, with an Historical Introduction*

returning criminal indictments, they just passed resolutions as Grand Jury presentments, denouncing the king and urging all Americans to support our war of liberation.

In early Massachusetts Bay Colony, a 'Court of Assistants' exercised most power in criminal matters; they made the laws and determined who should be tried. In March, 1634, the Massachusetts General Court issued an order to town meetings to select Grand Jurors, and the first regular Grand Jury in the colonies attended the Court of Assistants of Massachusetts Bay Colony in September, 1635.

So, town meetings elected jurymen to represent them on the first Grand Jury. At court, the jurors took an oath to present fairly all matters that came before them, then heard the charge of Governor John Winthrop. He warned the panel to report all crimes and misdemeanors that came to its attention…and told them to read the Ten Commandments. The jurors took their job seriously, presenting more than a hundred offenders, including several of the colony's magistrates.[16]

A Truly Independent Panel

In general, Massachusetts patterned its Grand Jury system after England's, but without the English method of selecting jurors because in England, sheriffs often abused their authority by selecting men who would charge offenses against certain persons and avoid charging others. Under the Massachusetts system, the clerk of the 'Court of Assistants' or of the county court sent warrants to the constables of the towns, requiring them to call a town meeting to elect the required number of Grand Jurors.

In one of his weekly Philadelphia law classes in 1790, which were attended by such notable leaders as George Washington, U.S. supreme Court justice James Wilson shot down the practice of Grand Jury having to rely on the prosecutor or the judge to give it instructions in who or what to investigate. Justice Wilson said that such an idea presented "a very imperfect view of the duty required of Grand Jurors." Wilson said that he considered the Grand Jury a vital People's check on all operations of government, and that every government office is

---

[16] Thomas Lechford, *Plain Dealing: or News from New England*, Massachusetts Historical Society Collections, 3:84 (1833) ; John Winthrop, *A Journal of the Transactions and Occurrences in the Settlement of Massachusetts* (Hartford, 1790)

within the aegis of Grand Juries, giving the People's panel an unrivaled ability to suggest public improvements and expose corruption.

Justice Wilson wasn't the first jurist to take that view. A decade earlier, judge Francis Hopkinson of Philadelphia denounced judges encroaching on Grand Juries. He said that from the terms of their oath, there was *"no bound or limit set to any number or sort of persons of whom they are bound to inquire."* Hopkinson also denied that judges could give directions to Grand Jurors. Note well: *the Grand Jury oath assigns no limit to their investigation other than their own diligence to seek out felony and capital crimes.*

In 1793, Treasury Secretary Alexander Hamilton instructed customs officials to report to him all violations of the neutrality laws. Thomas Jefferson protested strenuously against invasion of the province of Grand Jury, insisting that it would give bent officials authority to become criminal informers. Jefferson said that the advantage of the People's inquests was, *"a Grand Juror cannot carry on a systematic persecution against a neighbor whom he hates, because he is not permanent in the office."*

Citizen Presentments Are Vital

See the Shasta County, CA example at the end of the next chapter. If the Grand Jury is to be a real instrument of the People, then any citizen needs to be able to present a complaint to a Grand Jury. This is vital. In 1794, U.S. Attorney General William Bradford announced that citizens did not need to go through a committing magistrate to approach a Grand Jury with a *presentment* (see Chapter 7).

Remember, our system of law is a Common Law system and not a Civil Law system as in most of the world. But anyone who has read the laws of England as compared to ours will see massive distinctions between them. Where our Constitution calls for a Common Law interpretation, the colonists had a hard time deciding which Common Law to apply, England's or America's. Some American courts consulted and cited English decisions; others went so far in the opposite direction as to prohibit reading of any English authority in their courtrooms.

Due to the scarcity of published American case reports, more English than American cases were cited in American reports for a generation after Independence.[17]

---

[17] Lawrence M. Friedman, *A History of American Law* 110-15; 111-112 (1985).

But by the middle of the 19th century, Friedman relates, we had a truly distinctive common law system in America, with the first generation of American jurists creating a "separate language of law within the family founded in England".

And since criminal law was always largely state and not federal, those prosecutors who practice in the federal criminal courts look to the states, because state Grand Juries provide an unbroken chain of Common Law to instruct federal prosecutors.

Our Servants: Enemies of the People

American life has become controlled by lawyers and judges due to the People's sloth and abdication, and because the legal industry has worked steadily to kill off Grand Jury by first making it a rubber stamp, then coaxing corrupt state legislatures to hamper or kill it. I'm sure that state legislators fear losing their sweet deals, but We The People are fools to give up our most powerful law enforcement institution. For too long we've deferred to corrupt operators in legislatures. As former Stanford Law School dean Larry Kramer wrote, *"The supreme Court is not the highest authority in the land on constitutional law. We are."* [18] Given our Constitution, civics can be defined as simply: Who is Boss?

At TACTICAL CIVICS™, we consider ourselves missionaries. Our mission field is Americans who are ignorant of basic civics. Because they have no appreciation for the uniquely powerful U.S. Constitution, we start new members off by simplifying and clarifying terminology.

In 1951, the Kefauver Crime Investigating Committee of the 82nd Congress warned Americans not to rely on the government to control racketeering and organized crime in the United States. The Committee advised the people to use their local Grand Juries to arrest the corruption in their own communities. But by 1969, criminologist Donald Cressey's book *Theft of The Nation* presented over 400 pages of evidence that organized crime all but owned Congress and most of the state palaces. And that was over 50 years ago!

The Fifth Amendment requires that charges for capital and infamous crimes be brought by an indictment returned by a Grand Jury; so courts or legislatures can't abolish grand juries. But the federal system, by modifying Rule 6 in their Federal Rules of Criminal Procedure, just

---

[18] *The People Themselves: Popular Constitutionalism and Judicial Review*, pg 248.

stripped the federal People's Panels of their powers, turning them into rubber stamps for prosecutors. So of course, the big fish get away.

State Legislators Say, "Rights? What Rights?"

If you've never studied the clown show surrounding the Incorporation Doctrine, here is a quick layman's explanation before we see how state legislatures have run interference for the state's biggest criminals.

Incorporation means applying the Bill of Rights to not only Congress, but to state legislatures. When the Fourteenth Amendment was ratified in 1868, the U.S. supreme Court (SCOTUS) decided that the states should have to play by only a few of the same rules as Congress. Of course, the states are parties (representing We The People) to the Constitution but the SCOTUS is only a creature of that Law. The states, citing Amendment X, didn't want the federal court forcing them to do something not stipulated in the U.S. Constitution. But never forget Stanford Law School Dean Kramer's principle: *the U.S. supreme Court is not the highest authority in the land on constitutional law. We are!*

Every state legislature should be required to 'incorporate' every clause in the U.S. Constitution, to which they take an oath on taking office! In an 1884 case called *Hurtado v California,* the SCOTUS held that the Fifth Amendment (serious criminal cases must begin with indictment or a presentment by a Grand Jury) didn't apply to the states[19]. Since then, the state legislators get to decide whether We The People can still use our primordial institution of justice, the Grand Jury, to inspect and investigate potential corruption among our own employees!

SCOTUS never had that authority, regardless what John Marshall may have opined in 1803. Have five generations of government schooling rendered us so ignorant and compliant as to believe a legislature has that authority? Donald Cressey's 1969 book proved that congressmen, senators, state and federal judges, and even cabinet members up to that time were bent and bought. Can you imagine how much worse it is now? The People's Panel is our lifeline back to rule of law. We can't allow criminals to control school boards and city, county, and state governments. State legislatures have no authority to kill a *constitutionally-stipulated* law enforcement institution. How preposterous!

---

[19] The supreme Court first rejected 5th Amendment incorporation in *Hurtado v. California,* 110 U.S. 516, 538 (1884) and reaffirmed its ludicrous opinion since.

In the 1925 case *Gitlow v New York,* the SCOTUS decided that state legislators had to finally 'allow' their boss, the People, freedom of speech and the press. Only those two 'rights' of the Bill of Rights? In the 1943 case *West Virginia State Board of Education v Barnette,* judge Robert Jackson, writing for the majority, opined (note the underlined; that should read, "...to be applied by *Grand Juries.*")

> *The very purpose of a Bill of Rights was to withdraw certain subjects from the vicissitudes of political controversy, to place them beyond the reach of majorities and officials and to establish them as legal principles to be applied <u>by the courts</u>. One's right to life, liberty, and property, to free speech, a free press, freedom of worship and assembly, and other fundamental rights may not be submitted to vote; they depend on the outcome of no elections.*[20]

Remember our Hierarchy of American Government infographic on Page 10. Why do we allow the lowest-level servants below the line to steal the authority and sovereign powers of We The People, who live above the line? Because we were dumbed down by five generations of government schools, designed to produce unthinking worker drones for industry, who then generate tax revenues for bureaucracy. You see the system? If anyone in the private sector does this, it's defined in federal law and state penal codes as organized crime.

Good Guys Roster

By 'good guys', I only refer to this one issue; some of these states are rife with other corruption, but 22 states (AL, AK, DE, FL, KY, LA, ME, MA, MN, MS, MO, NH, NJ, NY, NC, OH, RI, SC, TN, TX, VA, WV) do not allow their judges or legislatures to abolish Grand Jury, either by explicitly denying the power, or by requiring that Grand Juries be used to bring charges for certain offenses.

Bad Guys Roster

Some of these states have excellent legislatures at this writing, but ten states' (CO, CT, IL, IN, IA, NE, ND, SD, UT, WY) constitutions allow their legislatures to abolish their Grand Juries. Only Connecticut did so; the other nine so far have only 'modified' it. Remember, *the People always retain the power to abolish any former amendment to their state constitution.* Tied

---

[20] *West Virginia State Board of Education v Barnette* 319 U.S. 624, 63 S. Ct. 1178; 1943

with Connecticut for worst corruption in this sense, Pennsylvania allows its county courts to abolish the use of Grand Jury to bring criminal charges, which is the only true purpose of Grand Jury. So of course every Pennsylvania county did so. But TACTICAL CIVICS™ chapters in Pennsylvania will make it a priority to push a constitutional amendment through to end that crime.

Seventeen states' constitutions (AZ, AR, CA, GA, HI, ID, KS, MD, MI, MT, NV, NM, OK, OR, VT, WA, WY) don't explicitly authorize abolishing Grand Jury but don't require a Grand Jury be used to return charges. In other words, they *implicitly* authorize its abolition. Strangest of all are the North Dakotans, who *require* that Grand Juries be used to bring felony charges, but give their legislature the ability to *abolish* Grand Jury! Do you see why you must pay close attention to those sneaky amendments to your State Constitution?

Taking it to County Level

Grand Juries have demonstrated repeatedly over the past century that they can effectively arrest centralized corruption in the name of the People. Today, Grand Juries remain the People's surest, strongest weapon against government corruption, including the blatant theft of elections by openly criminal big city political machines.

As we explained above, our system is based on the Common Law. In theory, we don't have a Civil Law system like Europe, with endless regulations, codes, fees, fines, rules, and taxes set in the law. But in reality, as Columbia law professor Philip Hamburger explains in his heavily-documented book, *Is Administrative Law Unlawful?* and his much smaller work *The Administrative Threat,* the Deep State is a massive, ever-growing cancer that gives Star Chamber type powers to unelected, unaccountable regulatory agencies whose very *existence* is illegal.

The issue of 'administrative law', a contradiction in terms, is beyond the scope of this Handbook but will be covered in our TACTICAL CIVICS™ Book Four, *The Banished Bureaucrat.*

This handbook is for members and foremen of *county* Grand Juries, not federal ones. Since the U.S. Congress is hopelessly corrupt and federal courts are creatures of Congress, the federal courts are a joke. Attorney Fred Bernstein noted that commentators disagree only on what to call the federal grand jury: "'indictment mill,' 'rubber stamp,' 'tool,' and 'playtoy' have all been suggested."[21]

The Banished Bureaucrat

Serving on a Grand Jury in your county is the most powerful position you can take in our court system, more powerful than that of judge; yet once we learn to take responsibility to enforce the U.S. Constitution, our authority to restrain and restore honest government extends far beyond our investigatory inquests.

The third of our 19 proposed reform laws is the *Non-Enumerated Powers Sunset Act.* The TACTICAL CIVICS™ proposed reform legislation will create a 7-member panel of the People in each congressional district, to review all federal agencies, bureaus, programs, departments, and regulatory nonsense. If they're not *specifically* authorized in the U.S. Constitution, a majority of the citizen review panels can vote to de-fund and shut them down. Forget politicians; who is boss in this Republic?

In *The Banished Bureaucrat,* we will flesh out this idea for this People's review panel in each congressional district called the Citizens' Volunteer Research Service, or CVRS. But let me just quickly outline it here, because besides our restoring Grand Jury and Militia in each county, getting our new Congress serving us back home and then establishing these review panels for the countless federal bureaucracies will be the most powerful control we will have exerted over these criminals in six generations. Bureaucrats in the 71 federal bureaucracies alone (omitting staffs of congressmen, senators, presidents, cabinet members, and judges) total 298,900 (rounded down to the nearest 100), vomiting out over 165,000 pages of 'regulations' each year.[22]

Since we elect 435 congressmen, 100 senators, president and VP, that means unelected predators and parasites on our backs unaccountably and invisibly outnumber 'servants' that we elect by 559 to one!

It's common sense: in America's highest law, read Amendment X. We The People stipulate that we retain all powers that we didn't delegate to government in the Constitution. But if that's the law, how do bureaucrats and other criminals in Washington DC manage to create

---

[21] Fred A. Bernstein, *Behind the Gray Door: Williams, Secrecy and the federal Grand Jury* (N.Y. University Law Review, 1994) pg. 563, 578
[22] Susan Dudley & Jerry Brito, *Regulation: A Primer,* pg. 5

thousands of agencies, bureaus, offices, project, programs and regulatory tricks and traps in clear violation of America's highest law?

Well, it *is* the law, sure; but We The People, who retain all imaginable powers for ourselves, do *nothing!* Now that will change.

Washington DC is an occupying power, eating up our substance and transmogrifying us into a northern annex of Mexico. We The People have lost millions of jobs to illegals and we're losing our rule of law and our entire civilization to organized crime, under the label 'government'. Isn't it insane? We've always retained the lawful power to stop this, yet the criminals do anything they like, with no authority to do it.

This is not a joke. Not even a nightmare; and it's not a hijacking. *It's organized crime.* We The People now must start arresting organized crime. That's what Grand Jury must direct its associated Militia to do. But we haven't done it because bureaucrats and corrupt payroll-skimmers from school districts to cities to counties to state and federal government offices – most of which we never authorized by law! – have trained us in alien civics and lies about who we are and what the law requires.

We may not even see this major reform in our lifetimes; perhaps our children or grandchildren will need to push that reform law through. But if we don't start taking our chores seriously now, beginning with oversight by serving on our county Grand Jury, our grandchildren will live under the control of organized crime and the parasites they bring from foreign countries to outnumber us.

When Obama vowed to "fundamentally transform America", he was as serious as Bubonic Plague. If we refuse to start doing our chores now, look at China, Russia or Venezuela; that's the life your grandchildren are doomed to live. Instead, let's make our corrupt servants get what they've been dishing out to productive America; let corrupt, feckless people go find real jobs.

Repentance begins with confession. This mess was entirely our own fault. 'We The People' is the highest office in American government; but during 160 years of ignorance, apathy, and sloth, we and our ancestors kept blaming the criminal servants while doing nothing.

The boss always has final responsibility. Remember that, each time you sign up for Grand Jury duty.

CHAPTER 2
County Grand Jury Ordinance & Website

County is the critical level, and our county governments should feel like We The People, Not 'them, the government bureaucrats'.

In light of the century of attacks on Grand Jury, the People's basic weapon to root out crime in public office and shield the People from revenge by corrupt government servants, TACTICAL CIVICS™ is bringing our County Grand Jury and County Militia ordinances *together* to our county governments.

Only by restoring both institutions do the People have a chance against the onslaught of organized crime, public and private. The overall county project is called Operation Restoration™. The Grand Jury restoration project is called Grand Jury Awake™ and the Militia restoration project is called American Militia 2.0™.

Let me be very clear that this will not happen in your county until your county chapter is ready to do it! That means that you've first gathered enough serious members to show up for regular meetings as described in Volume 1 of this 3-part handbook, and that your members know the mission plan and are reading and learning the civics. It may take two months, six months, or a full year before you reach that point. Please do not rush in to action before you are ready!

The leadership team is available for you seven days a week, almost any hour of the day. We must restore our land! But only on God's timing.

New Web Pages in Every County

The Operation Restoration™ roll-out plan is, at the same meeting of your county government, you will first have a spokesman for your county TACTICAL CIVICS™ chapter present the County Grand Jury Ordinance, shown in Appendix B. After that, at the same meeting, the area Militia's spokesman will present the County Militia Ordinance covered in Volume 3 of this Handbook.

As we explained in Chapter 1, we allowed our servants to build huge bureaucracies under our noses, make us pay for them, and then hide them out of sight. Now, we are going to change that.

In the brief Grand Jury ordinance, Article II, Section 5 reads:

> *The County shall make a page or pages available on its web site or prominently post links there, for County Grand Jury education, information, volunteer application with the County Clerk, and for Citizens to submit legitimate complaints of possible crimes, and calls for a Grand Jury if a panel is not sitting at that time.*

The County Militia Ordinance has a similar section calling for the county to maintain a County Militia web page or pages, to allow citizens to apply to serve in Militia and to announce training days, muster requirements, and important Militia contact information.

The Shasta County, California Grand Jury website <u>HERE</u> is a perfect example of how to do the website. Here is what its home page says…

Grand Jurors Needed – You Can Make a Difference

> *The Shasta County Superior Court is accepting applications from citizens interested in being members of the 2020-2021 Shasta County Grand Jury.*

> *The grand jury performs a vital independent citizen watchdog function over local public agencies such as the county, cities, school districts and special districts. It chooses its own subjects for investigation, publishes reports that highlight findings, and makes recommendations for improvements to the operations of these local government agencies.*

> *For further information on the Shasta County Grand Jury, see the Grand Jury Overview section below on this page. In addition, you can talk to former or current grand jurors, read prior reports by the Shasta County Grand Jury on this website page, or look at reports from other county grand juries on the <u>California Grand Jurors Association website</u>.*

> *To qualify, you must have been a resident of Shasta County for a least one year prior to service.*

> *You can download or print the <u>Grand Juror Application Form</u>.*

> *The deadline to submit your application is September 18, 2020. Be sure and fill out all parts of the application, including the required references and brief essay!*

Grand Jury Overview

The California grand jury system consists of 58 separate grand juries—one in each county—that are convened on an annual basis by the Superior Court to carry out three functions:

Investigating and reporting on the operations of local government (which is known as the 'watchdog' function)

Issuing criminal indictments to require defendants to go to trial on felony charges, and

Investigating allegations of a public official's corrupt or willful misconduct in office, and when warranted, filing an 'accusation' against that official to remove him or her from office.

The grand jury is well suited to the effective investigation of local governments because it is an independent body, operationally separate from the entities and officials it investigates. It conducts its investigations under the auspices of the Superior Court and has broad access to public officials, employees, records and information.

The grand jury's fact-finding efforts result in written reports which contain specific recommendations aimed at identifying problems and offering recommendations for improving government operations and enhancing responsiveness. In this way, the grand jury acts as a representative of county residents in promoting government accountability.

Do you have a concern to share with the Grand Jury?

Yes, I have a complaint

CHAPTER 3
How the People's Panel is Called Up

Venire pacias juratores was the ancient writ in Latin, from a king to his sheriff, "commanding him to cause to come from the citizens of the county, on some day certain, a certain number of qualified citizens who are to act as jurors in the said inquest". Over time, lawyers just began to refer to the Grand Jury roster as the *venire*.

Grand Jurors are normally drawn from the same pool of potential jurors as are any other jury panels, such as registered 'voters', motor vehicle owners, and public utilities billing databases. But a Grand Juror is not selected like a trial (petit) juror, who has to endure the *voir dire* process (there's that Latin again). That's a detailed interrogation by prosecution and defense counsel to weed out jurors who might be prejudicial to their case. In that respect, being selected for Grand Jury is simpler.

One major difference between Grand Jury and trial juries is that many states' legislatures require the county or superior court judge to call for a Grand Jury. Six states (KS, NE, NM, NV, ND, OK) passed laws stipulating that when citizens demand that a Grand Jury be impaneled, the judge *must* do it. But no law is required for that general principle; as justice Scalia explained (Appendix A), the Grand Jury is an independent body from all our servants (see pg. 34 discussion) to keep them honest.

What if the judge refuses?

Mandamus (yes, Latin…"we command") is a judicial writ; an order from a court to any government, lower court, corporation, or public servant to do, or to refrain from doing, a specific act which that body is obliged under law to do or to refrain from doing, and which is a public or statutory duty. So if your county judge is recalcitrant and refuses to impanel a Grand Jury, (s)he would become the target of an inquest by a Grand Jury summoned via a *mandamus* from a higher court, to which your group would appeal.

Technically, the state appellate court would *mandamus* another judge or even one of its own appellate banc to perform the duty refused by the recalcitrant judge. That is, instruct the county clerk to summon a panel of grand jurors. The offending corrupt judge would be the obvious target of that Grand Jury, once impaneled. In other words, it becomes the duty of the People of the county to assure that a bent judge is busted, and even if your state legislators say differently

I had a question recently from one of our members in Texas, who said...

> *I've been reading about the grand jury and militia in the TCTC; lots to learn... Went to the county courthouse in Rusk County; told the policeman I was here to sign up for the Grand Jury. First time he ever heard of anyone trying to volunteer. So I went to the district office to sign up. They said I can't do that; they have to pick from the roll. I asked them "What if I showed you the law that said I could sign up?". They said if I can show 'em, we can take it to the judge.*

This is definitely not the right way to go about it, as I am explaining, because this is a vital aspect of Grand Jury restoration. A county staffer opining that one can't volunteer to serve on Grand Jury is simply wrong. And saying, "we could ask the judge" is *very* wrong. Obviously, by such a tactic, a corrupt judge could shut down all honest, patriotic citizens interested in cleaning up their county.

The general principle is that whenever the public demands it, a judge *must* impanel a Grand Jury. This is the case even in the federal system. So, given the independence of the Grand Jury institution since long before the U.S. Constitution, the *People* must make the decision. Fine, but *how* do we make our desires known? Blog articles, letters to the editor, VFW bulletins...any way you can, your growing group must make known the truth when crime is going unaddressed in your county, and a Grand Jury *must* be impaneled whenever the *People* demand it.

Can I volunteer for Grand Jury?

Yes; but as of today, only if you live in one of 26 California counties. What about volunteering to serve in *your* county? Should your state legislators be able to shut down the People's only independent means of rooting out criminals in judges' robes, prosecutors' suits, behind sheriff's badges, or under a granite dome? *Of course not!*

There are some obvious points to be made here. First: a citizen cannot apply to serve on any *particular* Grand Jury panel – that is, on any Grand Jury panel investigating a particular defendant/target or case, or set of cases. Obviously, that practice would negate the entire institution, because a wealthy crime kingpin could have his hired minions just volunteer to be on the Grand Jury that would investigate the kingpin's crimes. In fact, that's been done by major crime figures with federal grand juries. But any citizen who has not been a convicted felon can and should ask to be placed on a standby roster at his county clerk's office, for Grand Jury service when needed, as described in Chapter 2.

Criminal law is the jurisdiction of the States, not federal government. As with every aspect of criminal law process, each state and *in this case each county*, has its own procedural details. But the fact remains that as a general rule, the People must always be free to volunteer to serve. That is one major goal of our historic County Grand Jury Ordinance.

Who Creates the Grand Jury Roster?

The panel for a particular Grand Jury will be randomly selected from a combination of the volunteer roster and the county's citizen databases (tax rolls, voter registration rolls). This is covered in the Ordinance; see Appendix B. (Grand Jury size and quorum per state, see Appendix C.)

As we just explained, only 26 California counties allow citizens to volunteer for Grand Jury; yet in Clause 61 of Magna Carta, Grand Jury was always chosen by the People themselves from among themselves. *We restore our system by willing citizens volunteering for Grand Jury service.*

Though the selection process itself for any GJ panel must be secret and random, at present in your county there is as little oversight of county clerk staff supposedly 'random' selection of potential Grand Jurors, as there is in your county of the ballot-counting process. Do you now see how our legal system is open to corruption? We have slept!

Our model County Ordinance on Grand Jury can repair these holes in the system. Your county TACTICAL CIVICS™ chapter will work to get the ordinance passed, once your chapter has grown to the point where it can pull together a big crowd to attend the meeting. Having a great plan is not sufficient; you must have great numbers to put the fear of God into your county servants.

Recap: Corrupt judges

Keeping in mind what we said on page 31 about corrupt judges, your state statute likely requires that no Grand Jury may be convened unless by the judge. Example: the Constitution of Washington State, Article I, Section 26 reads, 'No grand jury shall be drawn or summoned in any county, except the superior judge thereof shall so order'.

Yes, but even the rubber-stamp Federal Rules of Criminal Procedure recognize the primordial authority of the People over our own inquests. In its Rule 6, we read: *(a) Summoning a Grand Jury. (1) In General. When the public interest so requires, the court must order that one or more grand juries be summoned.*

So, such a state statute conforms to the U.S. Constitution, *only if judges respond to every call by the People for impaneling a Grand Jury when the need arises.* If your state has such a statute, it was likely a response to such groups as 'National Liberty Alliance', or money-raising show horses like Larry Klayman, seeking to invent a new concept: self-appointed, private 'grand jury' that seats itself.

On the other hand, the Washington State Constitution and any similar stipulations in state laws, together with Amendment V of the U.S. Constitution, establish an even clearer duty for a county judge to comply with all such demands, or be the target of an inquest by a Grand Jury summoned via *mandamus* by a higher court.

Recap: The People Are the Boss

At the bottom of every social ill in America, you can find the same principle: if the current law is corrupt, it became that way due to abdication of duty by the sovereign...the People.

In teaching TACTICAL CIVICS™ to our fellow Americans, if you ask, should not such a task be undertaken by some law professor or retired judge rather than a retired engineer, the question answers itself when you study the thousand-year history of Militia and Grand Jury. These are not for the crown's professionals, but are the *People's* institutions of law enforcement, ever since royal subjects began to make draconian demands of their kings.

Returning again to the general principle of American government, that the People are the apex sovereign, *if this is not the case in your county, your chapter should get this Ordinance passed* in your county government, to assure that any non-felon citizen who wants to volunteer for Grand Jury service, is welcome to do so.

Capital or otherwise infamous crimes are the aegis of the *People,* through the Grand Jury institution, which is *not* a function of the court itself. To the degree it ever becomes controlled or directed by the court, to that same degree it is being hijacked or commandeered by the court, which itself would be an infamous crime.

Thus you see that, like the Militia, the People's institution is both their offensive and defensive aegis (protection, sponsorship, direction, control). Even the federal system admits it: *"A Grand Jury is able to vote an indictment or refuse to do so, as it deems proper, without regard to the recommendations of judge, prosecutor, or any other person. This independence from the will of the government was achieved only after a long hard fight"*.[23]

The writers of the Federalist Papers constantly reiterate the People's sovereignty, as do countless opinions of the U.S. supreme Court during the first century of the institution's existence.[24] But the People remain clueless; we think ourselves powerless because that's what ignorant and lazy people do, as I learned from living 47 years on the Mexico border.

As I suggested before, never forget the graphic of our Hierarchy of American Government, on Page 10. The shorthand for that graphic would be, *"We The People, collectively, are sovereign in this Republic".* A general rule in terms of public actions with Militia and Grand Jury: *When trouble arises, Grand Jury and Militia are the natural and lawful solution, provided they work together, and the People sincerely and peacefully seek only to enforce the Law of the Land against any who appear to be violating it.*

The Page 10 Hierarchy of American Government graphic, the accurate portrayal of our system of government, should be the most common device you use to awaken those to whom our missionary institution is called to teach, support, and organize. Note how the Grand Jury and the County Militia reside at parity? Both are under 'We The People', which means the responsible community of citizens in any county.

---

[23] Admin Ofc of the U.S. Courts, *Federal Grand Jury Handbook.*
https://www.mdd.uscourts.gov/jury/docs/federalgrand.pdf
[24] Perform an online search for the first vital U.S. supreme Court case, *Chisolm v. Georgia;* read the opinions by chief justice Jay and associate justice Wilson.

We The People – the productive, law-abiding People – must escape our century-long hijacking by an arrogant, lawless legal industry and 'lawmakers' who transmogrified our society into a machine to produce trillions of dollars in revenues for the most unethical, treacherous, tricky 'professionals' in our midst. Lawyers pretend to complain about the corruption of judges and sheriffs, and they join in making lawyer and politician jokes. But criminals are no joke; this hijacking must end.

Stop Fearing Your Servants

If a bully who's a criminal struts down the sidewalk in a black robe, will that cause you to fear him more?

You and I must overcome our fear of arrogant, tyrannical judges, to put those servants back in their place in society, as ancient Britons did to arrogant, imperious kings. Remember this when you see a black robed tyrant trying to pull a fast one on you while you are serving on Grand Jury. A judge is the servant of the Law and of the People, and certainly no emperor on our payroll, sitting on a throne in that opulent building that we also pay for. *When you serve on a Grand Jury, your office is entirely independent of the office of the judge.*

Always remember your authority and duty. This is the only way out of America's self-destruction. Someone has to be responsible. Someone has to have the courage of their convictions and faith in God, to not be cowed by arrogant servants. *That someone can now be you.*

And when you serve, please brief your entire Grand Jury panel. This Handbook and our TACTICAL CIVICS™ website resources are your tools to lead others to a responsible new way of life. Given what's coming, this duty will serve America much more than if you were 'deployed' in some foreign country, killing people and breaking things.

After your first Grand Jury service, you will begin to realize why our Constitution demands this 1,000-year-old weapon of the People against tyrants and scoundrels…and why judges, lawyers, and their member organizations and lap dogs in state legislatures have tried so hard to kill it. The corruption of our legal system has been the subject of countless books, articles, websites, speeches, and whistleblower efforts. In some counties, the most arrogant criminal is the county judge himself or herself. The only way to arrest this corruption is the Grand Jury.

Illustrating how corrupt the states' judge-and-lawyer racket has become, journalist Edward Jay Epstein served for just one month on a New York Grand Jury in 2000 and gave a scathing report on the corruption in an article entitled, *Thirty Days On The Grand Jury*:

> *More importantly, even though the Grand Jury, through its inquisitory powers, is supposed to be the "exclusive judge of the facts," there is a Catch-22. It is not allowed to directly question witnesses. When a Grand Juror wants to ask a question, he must call over the prosecutor, and ask him to relay his question to the witness. The prosecutor may ignore or disregard the question if he judges it irrelevant. Prosecutors, in other words, are not obliged to ask Grand Jurors' questions that may elicit answers that confuse their case with what they consider irrelevant information. Since they, and they alone, are the judge of what is relevant, the supposedly-independent inquisition does not have independent means to question the prosecution's case.* [25]

How can a Grand Jury investigate criminal activity in government if the very servants they're investigating, control who is on the Grand Jury, what instructions they're given, what crimes they can investigate or cases they can consider, and tells them what they can and cannot do during their term? That would be ludicrous; like allowing the fox to guard the chickens. Yet it's precisely how most counties allow prosecutors to run the People's Panel today…all because Americans are ignorant of basic civics and history.

Again: read the excellent ruling in *U.S. v Williams* by the late justice Antonin Scalia; Appendix A. He described what we are *supposed* to have; the thousand-year-old Grand Jury institution that the judge-and-lawyer racket has tried to kill in America as it did in England.

We The People – that means us – have the authority to restore Grand Jury in our county, stronger than ever. And because all politics begin locally, *that is how we restore our Republic.*

---

[25] E.J. Epstein, *Thirty Days on the Grand Jury: The Torment of Secrecy.*

CHAPTER 4
Term, Authority & Duties of Grand Jury

Like everything else in this Republic of sovereign States, the terms, rules, and duties of their Grand Juries are *literally* "all over the map". Various states have different numbers, but a common arrangement is: 16 to 23 people are selected and 12 members of the panel have to vote. See Appendix C for Grand Jury size, quorum, and officers in your State.

Sin exists. If Grand Jury has not been impaneled in your county as long as you can remember, you should wonder if your county servants are more corrupt than average; especially judges and prosecutors.

Such conditions exist in states in which the legal industry has used your state legislature as its lap dog to leave Grand Jury technically in existence but only a rubber stamp of prosecutors and judges. Or worse yet, they pass 'laws' giving the Grand Jury all sorts of pointless busy-work. We'll discuss those below. But realize that your Grand Jury Panel has the authority to look into any public servant's office and operations that you either think is corrupt, or have received tips about, or even to assure yourselves that they are not corrupt! See Appendix A; Justice Scalia knew this fact, but We The People have not! *Until now.*

Yes, sin exists; so the most powerful white collar criminals own the judges and legislators, who make Grand Juries spend all their time on misdemeanors and penny-ante private-sector crime while the big fish are protected by bent judges and prosecutors who keep Grand Juries busy and distracted so they can never investigate serious crime.

Some states substitute a *clearly unconstitutional* preliminary hearing for felony and fraud cases; a judge decides whether a serious criminal case proceeds to trial without Grand Jury input; other states allow *the prosecutor* to choose a Grand Jury or a preliminary hearing. In those states, bent judges and prosecutors have it made. Grand Jury must be truly independent of the court, as history illustrates and as Scalia reminded us in his *U.S. v. Williams* opinion (see Appendix A).

For generations, GOP front organizations have offered popular 'Constitution Appreciation' courses, but have done nothing to train and organize citizens to *enforce* it. So public servants who take an oath to obey it, operate behind closed doors as though it doesn't exist.

Still, We The People are to blame. We abdicated our duty to root out crime by serving on Grand Jury; we must repent! In Chapter 2 we explained how We The People get our county government to enact our ordinances restoring the People's law enforcement when your state legislature has slithered like a serpent around the Constitution. As supreme Court Justice Chase wrote,

> *There are certain vital principles in our free Republican governments which will determine and over-rule an apparent and flagrant abuse of legislative power; as to authorize manifest injustice by positive law; or to take away that security for personal liberty, or private property, for the protection whereof the government was established.*[26]

Translation: The People through Grand Jury and Militia can overrule state or county legislators' flagrant abuse of law-making power, because we establish government to secure our liberty and property, not pass unconstitutional or crooked 'laws' and 'ordinances'.

> *The Grand Jury was an agent of the community, not simply an agent of the defendant. "[T]he Grand Jury's role [was] to represent the local community and thus act more independently of all the instruments of central authority, including the state or national legislature." The Grand Jury served to check the legislature by its power not to follow the law and not to indict people under the law.*[27]

Duration of Grand Jury Terms

Thirty-eight states (AL, AK, AZ, CT, FL, HI, ID, IL, IN, KS, KY, LA, ME, MD, MI, MN, MO, MT, NE, NV, NJ, NM, NY, ND, OH, OK, OR, PA, RI, SD, TN, TX, UT, VT, VA, WA, WV, WY) specify a term of their Grand Juries, which vary widely. The briefest is North Dakota's 10-day term; the next briefest term is Kentucky's 20 days. In Hawaii,

---

[26] Calder v. Bull, 3 U.S. (3 Dall.) 386, 388 (1798)
[27] Thomas, S. A. (2014). *Blackstone's Curse: The Fall of the Criminal, Civil, and Grand Juries and the Rise of the Executive, the Legislature, the Judiciary, and the States.* William & Mary Law Review, Vol. 55, Issue 3, pg. 1213.

Michigan, Nevada and Wisconsin, the Grand Jury's term is a year. In Florida, Illinois, Rhode Island, South Dakota, Virginia and West Virginia, it's 18 months. The longest terms are two years, in Nevada, Oklahoma, and Utah.

Then, in AL, ME, MD, NE, NY, RI, TN and TX, they impanel Grand Juries to serve during the term of the court that impaneled them. The panels may only meet occasionally, depending on what the Grand Jurors thinks it needs to do. But note well: *no panel should allow the judge or prosecutor to 'coach' the Grand Jury on what it can investigate, or suggest to the panel, "You can go home; we don't have anything for you."* Nonsense; as justice Scalia notes in Appendix A, the Grand Jury is the *People's* Panel of inquest; not the court's. Whatever investigations a Grand Jury thinks need to be made, that's what the panel will do, and court staff must render all necessary services for any such investigations.

AK, AR, MS, MT, NV, NJ, OH and OK use a variable term; a specified range of months "or until discharged". But remember: the Panel is supposed to determine when it is finished. Some states that convene for a term of a specified length allow them to be 'discharged' before the end of term, if there's nothing being brought before the Grand Jury. But once impaneled, *theoretically,* no judge or legislation can dissolve a Grand Jury in the middle of an inquest until it has no more to investigate, even if the panel's 'term' ends.

Having said that, this common sense and common law prerogative of the People's Grand Jury has never yet been tested in court.

Individual Juror Terms

If you live in these ten states (AR, CA, CO, DE, IA, MA, MS, NC, SC, WI), they specify length of time a Grand *Juror* must serve, rather than stipulating the length of the Grand *Jury's* term. The periods they specify vary widely. Massachusetts requires 4-6 months of service; North Carolina, 2-15 months; California, Colorado, Iowa and Wisconsin require a year (but CA requires only 30 day terms for criminal Grand Juries); South Carolina requires two years.

This is also a usurpation by our servants; if your state constitution includes an amendment that added Grand Juror terms, you should fight to repeal that preposterous rule. The state legislature has no authority to tell the People how long they must serve on the People's Panel; by rights it is entirely up to the Panel itself if a member must be excused.

Georgia and New Hampshire use both the Grand Jury term *and* Grand Juror service, one for regular Grand Juries and the other for Special Grand Juries.

Grand Juries do not typically convene daily[28]. Most often once weekly; even a few times per month in very low-crime counties, depending on how many presentments the panel receives. In states with long terms, Grand Jurors tend to be self-employed, retired, or others whose schedules allow them to commit the time needed.

Authority & Duties

The original purpose of the Grand Jury was to act as a buffer between the king (and his prosecutors) and his subjects. Before our War for Independence, colonial Grand Juries essentially ran local government, supervising everything from road-building and bridge maintenance to operation of local jails. Over the years, they lost much of their public affairs function as the operation of local government was taken over by bureaucracies, just like those that the colonists had left behind in the corrupt Old World.

Critics argue that this safeguarding role has been erased; that the Grand Jury simply acts as a rubber stamp for the prosecutor. But that's only because the federal courts have become so lawless and bossy, and because you can always count on a person on a public payroll to try to justify his salary while making his job as easy as possible.

As soon as you take that oath, you and your fellow members become the most powerful force for good in your county's court system. Your authority is equal to that of the judge or sheriff, and superior to that of the prosecutor. Remember this as you walk around in the county courthouse like you rule the place, because legally you do. That should not create hubris or arrogance, but a deep sense of responsibility.

The Grand Jury *is independent from the courts,* and the judge does not preside over it; merely impanels the Grand Jury. Appendix A is a brief but cogent explanation by the late U.S. supreme Court justice Antonin Scalia, explaining the independent nature of Grand Jury. As he noted,

---

[28] California is an exception; their Grand Juries work full-time during their terms, as mere efficiency panels. Seldom do they take criminal cases (the purpose of Grand Jury!) but when they do, they call that panel a 'Special Grand Jury'.

the function of the Grand Jury is to discover possible criminal activity, *or even to assure that criminal activity is not occurring in the county.*

With these things in mind: realize how long you have thought, "This corruption needs to end; somebody should do something". Well, now you are that somebody; and every staffer on the county's payroll works for your Grand Jury. Do not hesitate to use their services! But when being presented with a so-called 'information' by the prosecutor, always keep your defenses up. Use common sense and your own life experience. As we mentioned, referring to Richard Younger's now out-of-print book *The People's Panel,* Grand Juries have initiated some of the most important criminal cases in the history of our Republic.

I repeat my prior charge to you: <u>Never, ever fear a judge.</u> When on a Grand Jury, you are his equal in that building. A critical aspect of We The People taking back our rule of law and cleaning up our courts is retraining judges in due deference to the People, whom they serve:

> *We (judges) have no more right to decline the exercise of jurisdiction which is given, than to usurp that which is not given. The one or the other would be treason to the Constitution.* [29]

When serving, do not allow the prosecutor to rush your deliberations or attempt in any way to dissuade you from following up complaints by members of your community, or about which your own Grand Jury members have personal knowledge. If the prosecutor is presenting you with a case, let him make his explanation of the evidence, testimony, and felony statutes that appear to be violated. When he is finished, graciously but firmly instruct him to leave the chambers and let your Panel do your work. *You must realize that your Panel is equal to the judge.*

The whole purpose of 'the People's Panel' is to allow crime no hiding place, especially enablers in public offices who take a cut of the action. The Grand Jury has the duty to review evidence, whether it obtains the evidence on its own, from a citizen informant, a witness, or from a prosecutor or law enforcement staff. As a Grand Juror, you should avail yourself of all county staff: investigators, prosecutors, clerks – and runners to handle your Panel's menial chores and errands.

---

[29] *Cohen v. Virginia,* 6 Wheat. 264 (1821); *U.S. v. Will,* 449 U.S. 200 (1980)

Your duty is to determine whether probable cause exists to return a criminal indictment against the target(s) of your inquest, whether the case was initiated by the prosecutor and staff, or by paid law enforcement, or by your County Militia (if you have one), or your own panel created the presentment to launch the investigation. The one rule to remember is that the entire future of our legal system depends on citizens taking seriously our duty, our authority, and our opportunity for good when on a Grand Jury.

You may deliberate in your Grand Jury chambers, but that entire courthouse and staff belong to you while you are serving on a Grand Jury.

To review: the Fifth Amendment to the U.S. Constitution requires a Grand Jury indictment for any "capital or otherwise infamous crime". A capital crime means one punishable by death. An infamous crime involves fraud or dishonesty – such as the actions of countless suspects in Democrat-controlled counties in perpetrating Election Steal 2020.

Superintending Your State Legislators

The federal system can't abolish Grand Juries; but as we explained on pages 26-29, *state legislators are the most powerful enablers of criminals, by writing unconstitutional laws attempting to sideline the People's Panel.* They write legislation allowing prosecutors to avoid indicting big fish, using the excuse, "Grand Juries don't know how to run an investigation. They are slow, inefficient, and expensive to the taxpayers." In truth, a Grand Jury might indict their friends who are destroying America.

Perform an Internet search for your state's Grand Jury statutes and especially amendments to your state Constitution. Legislators love to hide their corruption in amendments that *they can later blame on the People for approving.* This is the game of politics; after generations of increasing corruption, America's courts have become alarmingly like those of European countries that have never known Grand Jury.

Imagine, if the People realized what they were reading, would they approve an amendment constraining the People themselves from inspecting their employees operations and expenditure of the People's money? They take our money, run expensive campaigns, head for the state palace to consort with the powerful, then seek to keep their boss, the People, from discovering the lawless activities of their friends in top local and county positions! *Who is the boss and paying the bills here?*

A Grand Jury has the authority to compel witnesses and subjects to produce documents and other evidence. It has the authority to compel sworn testimony of witnesses, including subjects of its inquiries.

It's difficult for a corrupt or conspiring witness to lie effectively when the witness doesn't know what the Grand Jury knows, or what the eventual charges might be. Too many people think of Grand Jury only in its 'shield' function for people falsely accused by corrupt or overzealous prosecutors. But the even more necessary function of Grand Jury today is to root out criminals in the county's legal system itself, or private-sector criminals who are 'too big to indict' or who have paid off law enforcement, prosecutors, judges, or all three.

Since the Grand Jury can subpoena witnesses and documents from any person or organization that the inquest panel suspects of criminal activity, the Grand Jury is society's most powerful tool against organized crime, terrorism, financial fraud, and corruption in school district, city, county, state – *and even federal offices, if the crime is committed within the state, against state residents.* The ploy of federal 'removal jurisdiction' is not available for criminal, only civil, infractions.

Your Investigations

As noted earlier, Grand Juries traditionally investigated both criminal activity and regular conduct of public servants' functions and departments. State Grand Juries retain these functions, but several state legislatures 'outsource' the People's ancient investigating institution to city, county, and state staffs themselves! Of *course* the foxes will care for the chickens! No problem!

As a matter of constitutional law, Grand Juries in every state can investigate suspected criminal activity. Yes, even in Connecticut and Pennsylvania, which eliminated the 'indicting Grand Jury'. How could the People of Connecticut allow their legislature to replace the citizen Grand Jury with 'investigating grand jury' made of one to three judges? *By definition, that is not a Grand Jury.*

Pennsylvania still convenes Grand Juries composed of citizens, but not to indict felons! In AZ, FL, LA, MN, MO, MT, and NC, Grand Juries can only investigate criminal activity brought to their attention by a prosecutor or judge! "Move on, citizen; nothing to see here!"

Grand Juries in AL, AK, AR, CA, ID, IN, IA, KY, NE, NV, ND, OH, OK, OR, SD, TN, TX, VA, and WV can investigate any activity that appears to violate the criminal laws of the state as long as it occurs within their jurisdiction; usually the county in which the Grand Jury sits, unless it's a 'Special Grand Jury' covering multiple counties and usually investigating drug crimes or organized crime and they usually convene in addition to conventional Panels.

Though it should be the *prime* function of county Grand Jury in every state, Grand Juries in only ten states – AL, AR, CA, MN, MO, ND, NV, NY, OK, and TN – investigate county officers and staff. With Election Steal 2020 in mind: Grand Juries in AR, FL, GA, KS, KY, TN, and TX monitor elections and bring criminal charges against those whom they believe committed election fraud.

Grand Juries have become rare because the American People simply don't understand that it is our power and our public duty to check on our employees! This is so obvious to every private-sector employer; why do We The People, who employ all of these public servants, think that somehow public servants will superintend *themselves?* Consider the $23 trillion debt they've run up, and rising tax rates still insufficient to cover their constantly bloating public spending. What, do we think that these scoundrels will arrest *themselves?*

In a county where the average level of corruption exists, there are two types of Grand Juries. The first type are proactive; they know they're supposed to be checking on the hired help, no matter how 'high' their office. This type of Panel will send the prosecutor and law enforcement staff on carefully-considered errands to obtain records and other evidence to help the Panel decide if an office or servant is bent. The second type of Grand Jury is a rubber stamp, allowing the prosecutor to feed them whatever cases, subjects, evidence, witnesses, and charges the prosecutor chooses.

Incidentally, members of Grand Jury have certain immunities under the law. They can't be sued for defamation, for a Grand Juror "is not civilly responsible no matter how erroneous [the] findings or how malicious [the] motive. . . ." [30]

---

[30] *Oppenheimer v. Ashburn* (1959) 173 Cal.App.2d 624, 629.

Common Public Crimes

What about immunity for our servants, especially the ones in black frocks? Let me list common felony charges; I'll cite only the sections from the Code of Federal Regulations; your State Penal Code sections will vary by State and will read differently. These are some crimes potentially being committed by your state legislators and by judges, prosecutors, constables, sheriffs, and other employees in your county justice system. As the U.S. supreme Court has ruled,

> *No man in this country is so high that he is above the law. No officer of the law may set that law at defiance with impunity. All the officers of the government, from the highest to the lowest, are creatures of the law and are bound to obey it.... It is the only supreme power in our system of government, and every man who, by accepting office participates in its functions, is only the more strongly bound to submit to that supremacy, and to observe the limitations which it imposes on the exercise of the authority which it gives.* [31]

That ruling applies in spades today to governors who have gone off the deep end, making imperial edicts and having them enforced by lawless thugs in 'law enforcement' who are ignorant of the U.S. Constitution and the limits of our servants' powers, compared with those retained by the People. And to further push out of your mind the idea that a judge is your demigod, two more court rulings. I just want to make it clear who has higher authority between the People's Panel and a judge who considers himself above the law ('immune') and untouchable. First a federal appellate ruling:

> *There is a general rule that a ministerial officer who acts wrongfully, although in good faith, is nevertheless liable in a civil action and cannot claim the immunity of the sovereign.* [32]

And then this ruling from the U.S. supreme Court, which ironically applies to most of the judges currently sitting in the supreme Court itself, after the travesty of Election Steal 2020:

> *Any judge who does not comply with his oath to the Constitution of the United States wars against that Constitution and engages in acts in violation of the supreme law of the land. The judge is engaged in acts of treason.* [33]

---

[31] *U.S. v. Lee,* 106 U.S. 196, 220 1 S. Ct. 240, 261, (1882)
[32] *Cooper v. O'Conner,* 99 F.2d 135 (1938)
[33] *Cooper v. Aaron,* 358 U.S. 1, 78 S. Ct. 1401 (1958)

So now to the short list of felonies that our servants may be committing. It's wise to have this Handbook when serving on Grand Jury, and to have your fellow Panel members read it or buy one for about $5. Drawn from U.S. Code Sections 18 and 42, these are a few potential charges against corrupt public servants who have hijacked our rule of law.

Misprision of Treason: USC 18 §2382 *"Whoever having knowledge of treason, conceals and does not make known the same to some judge, is guilty of treason for contempt against the sovereign, and shall be fined under this title or imprisoned not more than seven years, or both."*

Bribery: USC 18 §201 *"Bribery of any public official directly or indirectly, gives, offers, or promises anything of value to any person to influence any official act."*

Conspiracy Against Rights: USC 18 §241 *"If two or more persons conspire to injure, oppress, threaten, or intimidate any person in any State in the free exercise or enjoyment of any right, they shall be fined under this title or imprisoned not more than ten years, or both."*

Deprivation of Rights: USC 18 §242 *"Whoever, under color of any law, statute, ordinance, regulation, or custom, willfully subjects any person in any State the deprivation of any rights, shall be fined under this title or imprisoned not more than one year, or both."* USC 42 §1983 *"Every person who, under color of any statute, ordinance, regulation, custom, or usage, of any State subjects, or causes to be subjected, any person within the jurisdiction thereof to the deprivation of any rights, privileges, or immunities secured by the Constitution and laws, shall be liable to the party injured in an action at law."*

Concealment: USC 18 §2071 *"Whoever willfully and unlawfully conceals, removes, mutilates, obliterates, or destroys, or attempts to do so, documents filed or deposited with any clerk or officer of any court, shall be fined or imprisoned not more than three years, or both."*

Clerk is to File: USC 18 §2076 *"Whoever, being a clerk, willfully refuses or neglects to make or forward any report, certificate, statement, or document as required by law, shall be fined under this title or imprisoned not more than one year, or both."*

Conspiracy to Interfere: USC 42 §1985 *"If two or more persons in any State or Territory conspire for the purpose of depriving, either directly or indirectly any persons rights the party so injured or deprived may have an action for the recovery of damages against any one or more of the conspirators."*

Neglect to Prevent: USC 42 §1986 *"Every person who, having knowledge that any of the wrongs conspired to be done or are about to be committed, and having power to prevent or aid in preventing the commission of the same, neglects or refuses so to do, if such wrongful act be committed, shall be liable to the party injured."*

As I said above, one helpful exercise for every Panel member, even before listening to the prosecutor's presentation(s), is to read and highlight their own copy of this Handbook so that all members of the Grand Jury understand that what has happened to our civilization is not magic, politics, or a long string of bad luck.

Criminologists, investigative journalists, military generals and former intelligence agents over 80 years have documented in countless books and 'whistleblower' white papers that all three federal branches and our state palaces have long been involved in *organized crime*.

Distraction and Make-Work

That being the case, what do state legislators do? Distract the Boss! And since the Boss has civics upside down anyway, let's make him run in circles, with one finger in his nose!

Instead of performing the traditional duty of Grand Jury, handing down criminal presentments and indictments, many state legislatures today 'allow' the People only to investigate civil matters. The most common is to inspect and report on operation and condition of local jails. The legislatures of AK, AZ, AR, CA, GA, ID, IA, IL, LA, MD, MN, MO, MS, NE, NC, NV, NM, ND, OH, OK, OR, SD, TN, and WY either *require* Grand Juries to investigate these institutions, or *allow* them to.

As if that level of arrogance by state legislators was not enough, some state legislators assign their Grand Juries specific tasks to keep them too busy to investigate potential felons. For instance, in Alabama, Grand Juries must investigate the county pension roster to determine who is drawing a pension without qualifying. In California, Grand Juries must scrutinize transfers of land that *"might or should escheat to the State of California"* and must also investigate certain non-profits. And you can guess who they pick on first: patriot, constitutionalist, and Christian non-profits, of course. Those who still may have scruples.

In Georgia, Grand Juries have to approve any proposed change in a county's boundaries and set the annual salaries paid to probate court judges, court clerks, and bailiffs. But that's not demeaning enough;

Grand Juries in Tennessee have to investigate any failure to comply with state rules on *vaccinations for dogs and cats* and Pennsylvania Grand Juries have to approve proposals for statutes honoring veterans!

As you see, state legislatures create asinine 'laws' and amendments to state constitutions with one goal: distract the People's Panels so they won't have time to investigate criminals in office or who control those in office. But besides Connecticut (unconstitutionally abolished the People's Panel), and Pennsylvania (made it a useless appendage), the winners in the make-work-to-distract category are Alaska and Nevada, where the state legislatures instruct Grand Juries to, *"investigate and make recommendations concerning the public welfare or safety."*

Make recommendations! What happened to the purpose of Grand Juries: issuing felony indictments? Americans allow our state legislators and governors to act as our masters, keeping us too busy to investigate their secret arrangements and indict criminals, because for generations, taxpayers have allowed state government to control education, like every Communist dictatorship. *Now our entire government is hijacked.*

We were all children once, but we can't afford to keep living as children forever. Once we know basic civics, we understand that being the only human agency *over* our Constitution, We The People really do have authority to fix this mess, *and our servants don't have to like it.* Grand Juries can begin hunting down treacherous legislators, the worst enablers of corruption in our states.

Presently, we run them out of office instead of hunting down their crimes and applying rule of law. Judges, sheriffs, and county clerks are also elected, so when the People discover corruption in our servants, we just vote them out of office to allow the thug to pillage someone else. That is not justice, and it doesn't end that criminal's career.

Keep Control of Your Chamber

When your Grand Jury Panel is in session, you can allow in your chambers the prosecutor, witnesses, interpreters, and a stenographer or operator of a recording device used *to take evidence.* But no person other than the Jurors may be present in your chambers while your Panel is planning, deliberating, or voting. *Don't allow staff, even the prosecutor or investigators, to fool or intimidate you into allowing them to stay in your Grand Jury chamber when you're planning, deliberating or voting!*

The Panel can ask for as little or as much of the prosecutor and staff's services as you like. But nobody other than the Jurors (and possibly an interpreter/translator for the deaf if you have a deaf person on the Panel or testifying) can be present while the Panel is doing its work.

Witnesses, Subjects, and Targets

When you serve on a Grand Jury, you must see your Panel, at least for the time you are serving your county, in a sort of 'superhero' role that has been banished from the earth by criminals, and only exists now in America. Corruption is your target and your nemesis; be prepared to be surprised or shocked as you represent the People – the 'owners' of the county – and look behind closed doors for signs of embezzlement, grand theft, financial fraud, conspiracy with underworld figures or petty criminals, and other treachery.

Again I reiterate: *sin exists*. Men and women are not angels, and America didn't reach this retrograde place by accident. Some people in public employment have spent many years learning the tricks of the trade; yet they can have the most charming words in public. Use common sense.

I will take one protocol from the illicit U.S. department of (in)justice: their categories of Grand Jury subjects. First is a **witness**; your Panel has no cause to believe the person has committed a crime, just a bystander who saw or knows something. On the other end of the spectrum is a **target**; a person against whom your Panel has enough evidence to hand down an indictment. Then there is a **subject**; a subject of your investigation to whom you send out investigators to collect more information and possibly subpoena evidence or testimony from.

In the next chapter, we explain why secrecy is vital for a Grand Jury to maintain. But please remember: you are not a trial jury and the rules of trial court don't apply. You have the authority to collect information, testimony, and material evidence from witnesses *without divulging who or what you are looking for.*

If a Grand Jury allows the law enforcement personnel that they send out, to divulge to witnesses in advance who is a subject, or what evidence they seek, the evidence and subjects could suddenly disappear. If the prosecutor allows his staff to warn witness(es) or tell them what they are looking for, that is a clear indication to your Panel that three things are true: 1) the prosecutor is bent; 2) your investigation must expand; and 3) you must request a new prosecutor. And *that* you *can* divulge to the press! [34]

Reaching an Indictment

The Fourth Amendment of the U.S. Constitution reads,

The right of the people to be secure in their persons, houses, papers, and effects, against unreasonable searches and seizures, shall not be violated, and no Warrants shall issue, but upon probable cause, supported by Oath or affirmation, and particularly describing the place to be searched, and the persons or things to be searched.

Thus, to decide whether *probable cause* exists to believe that specific persons have committed a major crime, for a Grand Jury inquest to issue a warrant for someone's arrest or to search or seize property, you need to establish that probable cause exists. Your Panel either has direct knowledge of the situation, or you obtain evidence and hear testimony presented by witnesses or by the prosecutor or investigator(s).

In most cases, the prosecutor submits a statement of proposed charges to your Panel. In other cases, your Panel will call or subpoena witness testimony based on suspicion that a major crime has been or is being committed; you issue subpoenas and search warrants to produce the witness testimony and physical evidence you need to determine whether a crime or crimes are being committed or appear to have been committed in your county. Unless you have an attorney with criminal trial experience on your Panel, you should of course ask the prosecutor to help your Panel decide what criminal charges apply. Again, *the Grand Jury can call for the services of any court staff or law enforcement personnel within the county to aid in your Panel's work. Do not be shy in this vital public service.*

There are three main elements the Grand Jury must consider when making or analyzing a case. If the prosecutor is bringing your Panel the case, first you must **judge the law** by determining whether you believe the law or charge is acceptable. So if someone is being accused of breaking a law against your conscience, or is completely outside the limits that We The People place on our servants in the Constitution, your Panel has the authority and duty to stop that prosecutor.

---

[34] If you discover that the subject or evidence disappeared, the prosecutor is the only one who could have warned them, because you do not allow any other people in your chambers when your Panel is discussing strategy, evidence, testimony, etc.

Secondly, when a prosecutor brings a case before your Panel with certain charges in mind, it's up to your Panel to **check that the charges are accurate**. Determining that the proposed charges actually fit the alleged crime is important. For example, if a prosecutor brings a case before your Panel seeking to indict someone for bribery or racketeering, make sure the evidence supports that charge. If it does not, the Grand Jury can modify the charges to a lesser degree (say, ethics violations if it's a public servant).

The opposite is also true; if the proposed charges seem too weak, the Grand Jury can seek more severe charges or add others to the indictment. Remember the whole purpose of a Grand Jury: you do not work for the prosecutor. When in that chamber, you are performing superintendence work for We The People, 'above the line'!

The third thing the Grand Jury analyzes is: does the evidence adequately support the accusation? In other words, do you have **probable cause.**

Once you have all the evidence you think you need, you allow the prosecutor back in. If the prosecutor agrees with your Panel's conclusion that you have probable cause to indict the target of a felony or felonies, he reads the charges aloud, and you issue a **true bill** (indictment). Your work on that case is finished. You go home, and perhaps move to the next case when your Panel next meets.

See Appendix C for quorum required in your state, to indict. If you cannot get a quorum to conclude that probable cause exists, then you issue a no bill (an *Ignoramus*). In Latin that just means "we do not know", not that your Panel are all dummies.

I reiterate: *Grand Jury service is not a trial and you are not convicting anyone.*

Your Panel handing down an indictment is not the same as convicting the target; that's for the trial jury to decide. You have done your part to maintain rule of law. You go home and are out of the picture on that case. But your case can get blown in several ways, if your target is powerful. When the prosecution gives the witness list to the defense team, those witnesses can be intimidated or worse. Say you issue an indictment; even if the prosecutor agrees and signs off, your key witness or witnesses will have to testify in the trial phase. If the prosecutor can't get your key witness(es) to testify, then nothing you received from those witnesses is admissible at trial. It's hearsay, and violates the defendant's constitutional right to confront accusers.

Other Operational Issues

Although this Handbook is the first of its kind and I don't pretend to be an attorney, that's as it should be. Grand Jury is not a function of court staff but of the People assuring ourselves that law and order are being upheld to the best of *our own ability to ascertain it.* If you have never served on a Grand Jury, or if perhaps you once did, but only as a rubber stamp for a prosecutor, this Handbook will brief you and the other members of your Panel. We The People must do our chores rather than allowing foxes to keep guarding our henhouse.

How independent is the Grand Jury?

The Grand Jury is independent, and the instructions given to Grand Jurors inform them they are to use their judgment. So do that!

In the *corrupt federal system,* a Grand Jury hears only cases brought to it by the prosecutor, who also decides what evidence to subpoena, which witnesses to call, which witnesses will receive immunity, and who also does the basic questioning, only allowing the Grand Jury members to ask questions at the end of each witness's testimony.

In the *corrupt federal system,* the prosecutor decides if there's enough evidence to seek an indictment. Occasionally, Grand Jurors might be asked if they would like to hear additional witnesses, but since their job is only to rubber-stamp what the prosecutor plans, it's all a silly show.

In the *corrupt federal system,* the prosecutor drafts the charges and reads them to the Grand Jury, as a rubber stamp mechanism. Thank God, none of this need be true in your County Grand Jury. The entire history of Grand Jury is that a responsible panel of the People determine for themselves, with no coercion from 'the crown', what possible felonies are being perpetrated in the county, and by whom, and what evidence and witnesses to subpoena and bring in for examination.

Who must testify before a Grand Jury?

Your Panel or the prosecutor can obtain a subpoena to compel anyone to testify before a Grand Jury, without showing probable cause because that's the *purpose* of a Grand Jury.

In most jurisdictions, your Panel does not even have to show that the person subpoenaed is likely to have relevant information. The person subpoenaed to testify is compelled to answer questions unless he or she can claim a specific privilege, such as the marital privilege, lawyer/client privilege, or the privilege against self-incrimination. And even then, as the U.S. supreme Court ruled:

> *Although the Grand Jury may not force a witness to answer questions in violation of the Fifth Amendment's constitutional guarantee against self-incrimination...an indictment obtained through the use of evidence previously obtained in violation of the privilege against self-incrimination is nevertheless valid.*[35]

Can a subject call in a lawyer?

No! And speaking of lawyer/client privilege: your Panel *can* compel the subject's lawyer to testify about a conversation with the subject if the conversation was related to an ongoing suspected crime or fraud by the subject. But to illustrate how criminals control state legislatures: a few states allow a lawyer to accompany the witness; some allow the lawyer to advise his or her client; and others allow the lawyer to observe the proceeding! Of course, this guts the Grand Jury's ability to make a case.

Can a witness refuse to appear before the Grand Jury?

Not without risking being held in contempt of Grand Jury that issued the subpoena to compel their testimony.

What happens if a witness is found in contempt?

A witness who refuses to testify without legal justification will be held in contempt and can be subject to arrest and incarceration for the remaining term of the Grand Jury. And a witness who testifies falsely may be separately prosecuted for perjury.

If Grand Jury doesn't indict, can the prosecutor try again, or is that double jeopardy?

Double jeopardy doesn't apply to Grand Jury. In practice, however, it is uncommon for a prosecutor, having been turned down by the Grand Jury, to try again. Or he may become the next Grand Jury subject.

Can a Grand Jury subject offer evidence of his own?

The subject of a Grand Jury investigation has no right to testify unless subpoenaed, nor any right to compel the Grand Jury to hear certain

---

[35] Justice Antonin Scalia for the majority, *United States v. Williams*, 504 U.S. 36 (1992)

witnesses or evidence. It's entirely the Panel's decision if a target requests the chance to testify, whether to allow it. But in no case should your Panel grant immunity.

Although your Panel and/or the prosecutor may refuse to present evidence submitted by a target, some states require that exculpatory evidence be submitted for the Grand Jury's consideration. Be sure to ask the prosecutor which is the case in your state, or look it up.

<u>What is a grant of immunity?</u>

A grant of immunity to a Grand Jury witness overcomes the witness's privilege against self-incrimination. Then the witness is required to testify and the prosecutor is prohibited from using that testimony or any leads from it, to bring charges against the witness. If a subsequent prosecution is brought, the prosecutor must prove that all of his evidence was obtained independently of the immunized testimony.

In practice, it's difficult to successfully prosecute someone for criminal activity they discussed in immunized testimony, unless the prosecutor already had a fully prepared case before the Grand Jury immunity was granted.

Many states grant witnesses *transactional immunity,* barring prosecution for a transaction discussed in the immunized testimony regardless of whether they have independent sources of evidence.

<u>Can the judge be in the GJ Chamber?</u>

No. After calling for the Grand Jury and impaneling them, the judge must stay out of the picture until the trial phase.

<u>What protection does a subject have against witnesses lying to the Grand Jury, or use of unconstitutionally obtained evidence?</u>

None. Once the target is indicted, their only remedy is to challenge the evidence at trial. A witness may assert the Fifth Amendment if they don't know if the prosecutor has presented witnesses who lied. The witness can't risk testifying contrary to those witnesses, for fear of being charged with perjury if the prosecutor doesn't believe his testimony.

Examining Witnesses

The prosecutor will advise the Panel in the proper way to examine a witness. It isn't rocket science, but until you have probable cause, one of your jobs as a Grand Jury is to make sure you are not divulging a subject's name in case they are innocent. So for instance, if the Panel thinks a felony has been committed in the Grand Jury's jurisdiction and the prosecutor has told you (or the Panel already knows) the name of the subject – or especially if you aren't sure when or how the felony was committed – the Grand Jury first has to tell the witness the subject matter under investigation. Then you ask questions relevant to the transaction in general terms, in such a way as to let you determine whether the witness has knowledge of the violation of a particular law by any person, and if so, who that person is. So you back into it.

This Field Handbook is designed as a call to a vital public duty, not a detailed Grand Jury procedure manual. Anything you want to know, the prosecutor will teach you; by law, that is one of his duties. Put any questions for the judge in writing; don't go begging your servant.

Summary Regarding Your Duties

This is a thousand-year-old system of justice. It worked when the Grand Jurors were half-illiterate nobles and bloody knights, and it still works today, when your Panel is likely to be comprised of Americans from every walk of life. This chapter was long and may have read like a law school text, but if you read this Handbook a few times, it will make more sense each time. We The People are the boss, and we must start acting like it. Very bad people have not been afraid to keep ripping us off and destroying our civilization. We can't be afraid to stop them.

As I said before, I believe that the hardest part of God's judgment is still ahead. Most Americans are still spoiled and lazy. God will not apologize to Sodom and Gomorrah, nor will He go lightly on this godless generation. War – especially in the spiritual realm – rages over this civilization. If Satan has a main conductor for his side, I think it's the Clinton and Obama cabal and their thousands of deeply committed minions in the alphabet agencies and other illicit offices.

But there is plenty of evil at work in Congress and all of our state palaces, too. The war ahead may become as existential and terrible as Lincoln's war was; yet God will not forsake His own. As for me and my house, we will serve the LORD, and we will perform what He requires of man: to do justice, love mercy, and walk humbly before Him.

What about you?

CHAPTER 5
Grand Juror's Oath & Maintaining Secrecy

The Grand Jury Panel is selected at random from the county roll and volunteer roster, and they head for the Grand Jury chambers. The only people present in the room during proceedings are the Jurors themselves, a prosecutor only when requested by the Panel, and a court reporter, who is sworn to secrecy. No judge, clerks, or other court personnel. The Panel elects a Foreman, who will preside over the meetings. The Foreman then appoints (or has volunteer) a clerk, to call witnesses, keep track of evidence, and similar tasks. When you need something from court staff, ask for it.

The following oath or something very similar is to be administered by the judge (or under the judge's direction) to the Jurors:

> *You solemnly swear that you will diligently inquire into, and true present-ment make, of all such matters and things as shall be given you in charge; the State's counsel, your fellows', and your own, you shall keep secret unless required to disclose the same in the course of a judicial proceeding in which the truth or falsity of evidence given in the Grand Jury room, in a criminal case, shall be under investigation.*

> *You shall present no person from envy, hatred or malice; neither shall you leave any person unpresented for love, fear, favor, affection, or hope of reward; but you shall present things truly as they come to your knowledge, according to the best of your understanding, so help you God.*

As you see, witnesses are sworn to keep their testimony secret, for obvious reasons. Secrecy is demanded of the Grand Jury to prevent escape of people whose indictment might be contemplated, of course. But also to ensure that the Grand Jury is free to deliberate without outside pressure, and to prevent subornation of perjury or witness tampering prior to a subsequent trial; to encourage people who have information about a crime to speak freely; and to protect the innocent accused from disclosure of the fact that the subject was under investigation.

Total secrecy surrounding this vital institution of the People is no light matter. If a criminal or cartel discover who is on a Grand Jury or who is providing testimony to the panel, that person's life is in danger.

> *Since at least 1681, secrecy has been an established aspect of Grand Jury proceedings. The Fifth Amendment requirement that no person be held for a capital or infamous crime unless on a presentment or indictment of a Grand Jury has been repeatedly held to imply that such Grand Jury proceedings be kept confidential from the public. American Grand Jury practice has generally required grand jurors to swear that they would keep their proceedings secret, upon penalty of contempt of court. The Supreme Court has described the Grand Jury as an institution whose purposes would be totally frustrated if conducted in the open.*[36]

Any witnesses called to testify, do it one at a time. Witnesses aren't entitled to have anyone else present, including an attorney. If the Grand Jury approves (but it need not do so), the witness may consult with legal counsel outside the hearing room.

Witness Oath Before each witness is examined, the Foreman or a person under the Foreman's direction must administer the oath to the witness (your state's may vary a bit): *You solemnly swear that you will not reveal, by your words or conduct, and will keep secret any matter about which you may be examined or that you have observed during the proceedings of the Grand Jury, and that you will answer truthfully the questions asked of you by the Grand Jury or under its direction, so help you God.*

The Panel and prosecutor question the witness. Not being a trial and no defense attorneys being allowed, witnesses aren't cross-examined. But witness testimony is given under oath, just as in a trial.

Grand Jury Chambers

To maintain secrecy and security, Grand Jury proceedings are private, conducted in areas not accessible to the public; a number of states have laws stipulating that requirement. A New Mexico statute, for example, stipulates that all Grand Jury deliberations, "will be conducted in a private room outside the hearing or presence of any person other than the Grand Jury members". To ensure that their Grand Jury proceedings

---

[36] Roots, R. (Fall 2010). *Grand Juries Gone Wrong*. Richmond Journal of Law and the Public Interest, Vol. 14, No. 2 (pg 351).

remain secret, a number of state laws stipulate that private rooms be made available for their sessions. Kentucky and North Dakota statutes, for example, put the burden on county officials generally to provide private Grand Jury chambers. Texas puts the obligation on the sheriff, while Mississippi puts it on the attorney general.

Again, because this is not a trial and your subject(s) may be as innocent as you are, do not speak about your investigations to anyone outside the Grand Jury chambers, and then only when the Panel is alone.

Once in the public trail phase, secrecy ends but the need for witness protection is recommended or mandatory, depending on the nature of the case, as the movie *16 Blocks* dramatically depicts. At one time, defendants in criminal trials were never given access to the Grand Jury testimony that resulted in the indictment. By the 1980s in most states, if a witness who testified before the Grand Jury was called to testify at trial, the defendant received a copy of that witness's Grand Jury testimony, for possible impeachment of the witness.

Most states also give the defendant a list of everyone who testified before the Grand Jury, and several give the defendant a full transcript of all relevant Grand Jury testimony.

CHAPTER 6
Taming Your County servants

In Chapter 3 we explained how citizens should deal with a corrupt judge who refuses to impanel a Grand Jury. One has to assume that in the vast majority of cases, the prosecutor is (relatively) honest. We will discuss below the case when your Panel received a tip that the prosecutor or any major county 'official' including the judge is committing crimes. But first, some basics about American prosecutors.

It may seem odd to most people today, but when our Constitution was ratified, there were no such things as public prosecutors in America. Prosecuting criminals was a gig for private prosecutors, who were either paid by the victims or their heirs, or by lawyers picked from a prosecutor pool on a rotating basis, like indigent defendants are represented today. But when cities (thus crime) grew too large, the prosecutor pool workload raised the costs of private attorneys to the point that they got courts to create an office of the public prosecutor. Jon Roland explains how potential for corruption is created:

> *One of the results of this has been that in most jurisdictions the public prosecutor is given a preferential role in submitting bills to the Grand Jury, and to managing the proceedings of it, something that is supposed to rest on the consent of the Grand Jury itself. Moreover, he is sometimes given de facto control over access to the grand jury by the public… The result is that, whereas during the Founding Era members of the public could easily submit petitions to the Grand Jury, often directly, for indictment or presentment, such petitions are now channeled through the public prosecutor and the Grand Jury is isolated from any matters the public prosecutor disapproves.*[37]

The united States form the only Republic in the world where the citizens elect prosecutors. As I mentioned above, American prosecutors began as private lawyers for victims. After the War for Independence, most states gave their governors, judges, or legislators the power to appoint prosecutors. Starting with Mississippi in 1832, states adopted

---

[37] Retrieved from Jon Roland's excellent website, www.constitution.org

new constitutions, statutes, or amendments that made prosecutors elected servants. By 1861, nearly three-quarters of the Northern states elected their prosecutors.

As Michael Ellis said in the only detailed study of the history of public prosecutors in America,

> [F]airness and efficiency concerns were largely absent from the debates over whether to make prosecutors elected. Instead, supporters of elected prosecutors were responding to governors and legislators who used the appointment system for political patronage. [38]

Ellis explains that as prosecutors gained power over criminal prosecutions, political reformers around the time of Lincoln's war believed it was crucial to remove prosecutors from partisan politics. Some hoped that elected prosecutors would be more accountable to the citizens and communities they served. But as Ellis explains, "not long after prosecutors became elected...(they) quickly became involved in, and co-opted by, partisan politics."

The lesson from all this is, as Lord Acton said, "Power tends to corrupt, and absolute power corrupts absolutely." Subjects of monarchs knew this very well, so in England's Common Law system, the People themselves developed their own defenses against powerful and corrupt office holders. In America, as Richard D. Younger surveys in great detail in his book[39], *The People's Panel*, the People in this country maintained a far more robust, far-reaching oversight of public office holders than subjects of monarchs had ever done in England. That is, until the legal industry hammered away at it until most Americans know nothing of our authority and duty to catch corrupt politicians.

Bent Servants High and Low

If there are only two things that you take from this Handbook, I hope it will be first, to burn into your memory the page 10 infographic; and secondly, remember that the most important investigations you can conduct are of public servants, especially state legislators who reside in your county, and staff in the justice system itself. Yes, it's a little scary, but hasn't it dawned on you that one generation after another, productive taxpayers just keep complaining about corruption but seem

---

[38] Michael J. Ellis, *Origins of the Elected Prosecutor* (Yale Law Journal, 2012)
[39] TACTICAL CIVICS™ is publishing a reprint edition of that vital, rare book.

to have no intention of actually arresting it? As Jason Hoyt wrote in his excellent book,

> *When was the last time you heard about a Grand Jury, out of their own initiative, beginning an investigation without being called by a judge or a prosecutor? Have you ever heard of that?*
>
> *Think about this for a moment. When the county commission votes on some new government construction and the cousin of the county commissioner in District 5 is awarded a no-bid landscaping contract, the local Grand Jury should investigate to see if there might be ethics violations in play.*
>
> *When the state passes a law that allows a local municipality to violate your property rights, a Grand Jury has the power to step in and act as a shield. When your congressman is being bribed by lobbyists to vote for their pet projects, your local Grand Jury needs to step in and hold them accountable.*[40]

A Grand Jury can decide to begin investigating the local government on suspicion of "fraud and dishonesty," an infamous crime. Our proposed County Grand Jury Ordinance will make it a simple matter for anyone in the county with evidence of a potential felony crime being committed or having been committed, to submit that evidence or testimony to the inquest. They can do so in a physical evidence packet, or by entering a complaint on the new web page area created for Grand Jury on the county's website, as 26 of California's counties already do. Regardless what your state legislators decided on their own, the People must decide that it's time to start dealing with criminals.

Stand Your Ground

If your Panel believes it has enough evidence for a true bill and the prosecutor disagrees with you, send him out of your chambers and have your panel consider: is the prosecutor compromised by political or power issues?

He may not be in cahoots, but here's how inside politics works on court staffs and in paid law enforcement: if paid county employees think that hauling in a particular politician or high-ranking public servant will cost them their job or advancement, the prosecutor will complain, "we don't have enough; I don't want to lose the case for indicting with insufficient evidence".

---

[40] Jason W. Hoyt, *Consent of the Governed,* from page 99

You are a thinking adult; use your head. Grand Juries for over 1,000 years have been comprised of regular citizens who see what they believe is crime, and issue an indictment against it. You don't have to bow to a prosecutor who is only protecting his own career or who, in the worst case, is a co-conspirator. Stand your ground, and hand down your indictment signed by the Grand Jury Foreman.

On the other hand, if the prosecutor presents your Panel with a case, you send everyone out of your chambers and deliberate the case considering all the facts, testimony, and physical evidence against the applicable Penal Code sections that the prosecutor is alleging. If your Grand Jury carefully considers the evidence and a quorum can't find probable cause, *stand your ground and do not indict.*

In our system of law, that decision is up to the Grand Jury and no one else. If you have ever served and you took your duty seriously, you know what an amazing thing it is when the People stand up and do the right thing. With preparation, when they take the duty seriously, regular Americans will make you very proud.

CHAPTER 7
Presentment, Indictment & Information

The Grand Jury is often called 'The People's Sword and Shield' because it works for the People to arrest the evildoer – that is the sword in the Romans 13 sense – and also as a shield to protect an individual against corrupt, vindictive, or overzealous government.

In the Fifth Amendment, We The People stipulate that, *"No person shall be held to answer for a capital, or otherwise infamous crime, unless on a presentment or indictment of a Grand Jury."* This means that when a person is in the process of being charged with a felony or serious crime, the People stipulate in the Constitution that it will be through a Grand Jury *presentment* or *indictment*.

Presentment

In criminal law, a *presentment* is a written notice by a Grand Jury of an offense, either from their own knowledge, from law enforcement, or from any witness in the community. In the early days of American common law, a presentment was the most common way for an initial public accusation to be brought against a corrupt public official.

Presentments were sometimes simply called reports, and called public attention to actions or inactions by public servants, whether or not they rose to the level of a capital or infamous crime.

Renee Lettow Lerner described how the federal law guild has destroyed the ancient presentment power of the Grand Jury in the federal system:

> *The history of federal Grand Jury powers is the story of descent into confusion. In emphasizing the Grand Jury's function as a shield against government oppression, historians have glossed over its use as a sword. Before the Constitution, the colonies relied heavily on grand juries to perform accusatorial, administrative, and even legislative functions. Early federal grand juries remained spirited and regularly issued presentments. In the twentieth century, however, Grand Jury law became murkier, particularly*

with the passage of the Federal Rules of Criminal Procedure. Lawyers and judges now doubt the existence, let alone the extent, of the presentment power.[41]

Indictment

We've discussed the *indictment;* the written charge of the Grand Jury that it finds probable cause for formal charges to be brought against the accused; that the charges are acceptable to the Panel and accurate enough to get the prosecutor's sign-off and send down for trial by a petit jury for that capital or otherwise infamous crime that appears to have been, or is being, committed. This is done with the aid and support – *but not the coaching* – of the prosecutor.

Information

A defendant who knows he's guilty, or who is being coerced by a corrupt prosecutor, may decide to waive the right to a Grand Jury. In those cases, an *information* instead of a Grand Jury indictment, starts the formal criminal justice process. An information is the bureaucrat version of a Grand Jury indictment, but without the Grand Jury. It is a document prepared by prosecutors. While a Grand Jury presentment is based on the direct knowledge of the panel members themselves or from honest members of the community, an information is based on police reports or other documents from law enforcement, or from statements of witnesses.

In civil cases, the plaintiffs bring what's called a *complaint*. In criminal felony cases, the Grand Jury brings an *indictment,* or in lawless states, the prosecutor brings an *information*. All of these documents need to include the pertinent details so the defendant can understand what charges are being brought against him.

The Deep State's all-out attack on the Trump administration illustrated how corrupt the DOJ and FBI have become. But even in the state systems, if a Grand Jury is not involved, law is by bureaucracy, Roman style. Charging documents are filed after a *preliminary hearing*. Even in felony crimes, the information route is the norm in too many state jurisdictions. This must change.

---

[41] Lettow, R. B., *Reviving Federal Grand Jury Presentments*. (Yale Law Journal, 1994)

CHAPTER 8
Subpoena & Warrant

When serving on Grand Jury, your Panel will issue two basic kinds of legal order, to be served by the bailiff, paid law enforcement, or your associated Militia if the case warrants. The two kinds of legal order are a subpoena, and a warrant. Warrants are further broken down as either a search warrant or an arrest warrant.

Subpoena

The subpoena is a process and also a piece of paper that is served on a witness from the Grand Jury Foreman, ordering a witness to turn over documents listed in the subpoena, or to appear and give testimony before the Grand Jury either immediately or at the time and date noted in the document. For obvious reasons, the Grand Jury does not name the matter under investigation.

In most states, the Foreman may issue a subpoena either when the Grand Jury is in session or in a recess period, and if the bailiff or other process server returns with the process and the Foreman is not in or the Panel is on recess, they turn it in to the district clerk.

Search Warrant

This one you have likely seen on television. It is a legal authorization from the Grand Jury (in some states must have approval of the judge) which states: your County Grand Jury name (and possibly the name of the judge); the subject's name and address; the date the warrant was issued; the description of the place(s) to be searched; the description of the items(s) being searched for; and the agency (sheriff, Militia unit, police) authorized to conduct the search. If the subject is a sleazeball politician and the sheriff's team or Militia unit agree to play it like the IRS does with conservatives, you can have them serve the warrant at 3 a.m., with six vehicles and bright lights on the subject's face.

Arrest Warrant

Also executed by the same law enforcement teams, an arrest warrant is issued when the Grand Jury has probable cause that the target has committed the felony or felonies and is a flight risk. It must contain the basic reasons why the Grand Jury has issued the warrant; must state that it's issued by the Grand Jury; and must contain specific description of the person to be arrested.

Again, if the subject is an imperious, corrupt governor or something and your sheriff's team or Militia unit agree to play it like the IRS, have them serve the warrant at 2-3 a.m., with six vehicles and bright lights on the target's face. And be sure to have conservative press and perhaps even a blogger there, as IRS does with CNN when arresting Trump's associates.

CHAPTER 9
Deploying Militia & Paid law enforcement

Given the many attacks on our communities and way of life – attacks from our own lawless servants in state palaces and Washington DC – there has never been greater need for *"Militia, to "execute the Laws of the Union, suppress Insurrections, and repel Invasions".*[42]

Regardless what lies ahead for our Republic, we can never go far wrong by returning to rule of law, and when the servants are in high rebellion, the People must have a plan to defend ourselves, our families, shops, farms, businesses, and communities. As Americans once did before, the American Heartland, if required, right here on our own ground will defeat the most powerful military on earth.

Even if the forces of Obamanation and the turncoat element of U.S. military are joined by Communist China or Russia, honorable American forces will join with Militias that will rise up overnight and we will fight to the death for our homes and families – *and win* – if it comes to that. But we must remember that America has been shaking her fist in God's face for generations. Read Essay #34 of our book, *A Republic to Save: Essays in TACTICAL CIVICS*™ where we provide links to six heavily-documented books exposing Lincoln as an agnostic and an admirer of and correspondent with Karl Marx.

American Communism is 160 years old and American Fascism is 110 years old. Will we repentantly begin investigating and arresting criminals who are willfully destroying our civilization, or would we rather continue under God's judgment? If we choose the former, we must assume that the Communists control a great many police departments and sheriff's offices, as cases over the past decade have demonstrated. Politics should not play into law enforcement, but paid careerists go with whoever writes their payroll checks. So at this point in the domestic gaslighting campaign, federal military may not be trustworthy.

---

[42] U.S. Constitution, Article I, Section 8, Clause 15

This is an admittedly tough situation to contemplate; but it's foolish not to consider the various scenarios that we may face in the near future, given the withering, ruthless, treacherous attacks launched by the Deep Axis since Trump went to DC to threaten the globalist cartels.

As for Trump, we've said many times that he is not our savior – indeed, no president ever can be. But he was the toughest fighter against the Deep State in my lifetime; more so than Ronald Reagan. So I heartily supported, and still support him. But with eyes wide open: he played footsies with Big Banking, Big Tech, Big Pharma, and the Sodomite lobby; he made disastrous cabinet picks and fired excellent people; and he led the Chinavirus circus month after month, making the murderous Mr. Fauci a celebrity.

On October 30, 2008 in Columbia, Missouri, Barack Hussein Obama said, *"We are five days away from fundamentally transforming the United States of America"*. This was on the heels of Bush II having already begun fundamentally turning these sovereign States into captive vassals of a police state. Only years later did America see how friendly the Clintons, Bushes, and Obamas were; the Deep Axis has allies worldwide, and they're powerful, ruthless people with plans for the world.

If We The People – those Americans still committed to Jesus Christ and the U.S. Constitution – do not take this 160-year-old domestic enemy seriously now, our grandchildren will see Mr. Obama's dream come true. Instead of the messy death of American Communism at last, they will be doomed to live through its new ascendancy.

Militia, in the American Constitutional context, is not simply Americans in arms and angry; that is anarchy and folly. In our Constitution, We The People only authorize one armed force, Militia, to execute our laws, put down insurrections, and repel invasions. As we learn to be the best Grand Jury members we can, others will be using Field Handbook Volume 3 to become the best Militiamen they can be. In good times and hard times, the two institutions must work together. We may need to initiate some very tough felony cases against our public servants, so TACTICAL CIVICS™ has made it a priority to bring the patriotic Grand Jury and its associated County Militia together, to restore our land by the grace of God.

CHAPTER 10
We The People (Home) Rule

In 2020, our Chapter Founder of the TACTICAL CIVICS™ Litchfield County Chapter joined me and co-founder John Leyzorek of West Virginia, to begin researching state Grand Jury in Connecticut, which led us to a discussion of Home Rule versus the silly chimeras known as *Dillon's Rule* states. This is an important argument that goes back as far as human civilization.

Connecticut is important to our mission for many reasons, not the least of which was that as a colony, its *Fundamental Orders* became the first written constitution in America (ca 1639), for which it is known as 'The Constitution State'. Connecticut established itself as independently-governed among the early colonies; an historical act comprising a significant foundation to Home Rule.

The "Rule" is Only a *Wish*

John Forrest Dillon was a federal judge who cooked up the 'Dillon's Rule' of top-down government that is favored by big-government proponents. Dillon was a favorite son of Davenport, Iowa, where I founded Morningstar Academy, a classical Christian school, over 30 years ago. In the town square is a large monument to Dillon, who lived and practiced law in Davenport for about 15 years, so they claim him, though he was born and died in New York.

Setting aside Dillon's infamy for philandering: what could possibly make *one* opinion by *one* federal circuit court judge in one case[43], become a universal rule for community self-determination in our republic? Well, *imperious lawyers,* that's what. One federal district court judge's opinion? Everyone knows that legal rulings in cases apply only to those fact and law situations and parties; they are *not* generally applicable. Basic logic says that if one judge's opinion in a case could

---

[43] *Clinton v Cedar Rapids and the Missouri River Railroad,* (24 Iowa 455; 1868).

constitute a new 'rule' of universal application, every sitting judge would become his own American emperor!

So please, let us call it *Dillon's Wish* from now on; a more fitting label for a state's arrogation of every community's right to govern itself. As I have often reiterated, Granite Dome Syndrome can give a politician such arrogance as you would not believe, unless you've spent time in your state palace trying to talk sense to that dangerous species.

James Madison on Home Rule

In our mission, we constantly strive to erase the term 'nation' and train ourselves to use the accurate label for these united States: a *Republic*.

In Federalist #39, James Madison opened the home rule discussion:

> *The idea of a national government involves in it, not only an authority over the individual citizens, but an indefinite supremacy over all persons and things, so far as they are objects of lawful government. Among a people consolidated into one nation, this supremacy is completely vested in the national legislature. [But] among communities united for particular purposes, it is vested partly in the general and partly in the municipal legislatures. In the former case, all local authorities are subordinate to the supreme; and may be controlled, directed, or abolished by it at pleasure. In the latter, the local or municipal authorities form distinct and independent portions of the supremacy, no more subject, within their respective spheres, to the general authority, than the general authority is subject to them, within its own sphere.*
>
> *In this relation, then, the proposed government cannot be deemed a national one; since its jurisdiction extends to certain enumerated objects only, and leaves to the several States a residuary and inviolable sovereignty over all other objects.*

Madison is saying that in our Republic, government has only such powers as we enumerate in constitutions. There can be only one King of the Hill in constitutional hierarchy, and as we stipulate from the first words to the last words of the U.S. Constitution (and remember our infographic on pg 10), We The People are the top government 'office' and the sovereign power in America. But do we *enforce* those constitutions when our servants go berserk?

The late atheist historian Edmund S. Morgan, in his book *Inventing the People,* suggested that the phrase *We The People* has always been held as more of a romantic nostrum rather than real, operating law. Nonsense.

TACTICAL CIVICS™ is a commonsense mission to help Everyman cut the Gordian knot created on one hand by the historic mob actions surveyed in professor Christian Fritz's book, *American Sovereigns,* and on the other hand, the popular constitutionalism proposed in Stanford Law School dean Larry Kramer's 2004 book, *The People Themselves.*

In his 2008 work, Mr. Fritz struggles for 400 pages to arrive at a consistent thesis, citing and parsing three mob actions in early American history, describing the reactionary nature of these uprisings but never touching the core question of We The People actually *enforcing* the U.S. Constitution.

Mr. Kramer did a fine job of asserting and defending his thesis: We The People hold the sovereign office in American constitutional law. He repeatedly disrobes and excoriates his former profession and the U.S. supreme Court (SCOTUS) in particular, and cites long custom, law, rulings and tradition in support of his thesis. But while he shows how far off the rails our legal servants have run, he never touches on how We The People might actually begin to enforce the U.S. Constitution.

The late Mrs. Phyllis Schlafly wrote in the same year as Larry Kramer's book, a wonderful 150-page book called *The Supremacists: The Tyranny of Judges and How to Stop It.* She reminds us that We The People stipulate in Article III, Section 2, Clause 2 that we grant Congress plenary authority to strip subject matter jurisdiction from any federal courts including SCOTUS. See Section 2 of our proposed Constitutional Courts Act on pages 255-256 of *A Republic to Save;* we cite seven SCOTUS opinions acknowledging Congress' power over the court.

'Constitutionalists' including law professors who insist that the only way to throttle back the lawless SCOTUS and inferior federal judges is to elect a 'constitutionalist' president to replace SCOTUS judges, should have failed Constitutional Law.

Self-determination, in worst case scenarios, must go back to root stock, which we have done. Our county ordinances for Grand Jury and Militia, as authority cite the Declaration of Independence, James Madison, and Antonin Scalia.

Home Rule: the Common Law Default

Here in my state of Texas[44] about 94% of towns over 5,000 residents are *Home Rule* communities. But because the primordial Spanish law of land grants and municipalities held true in most of these united States before 1800, you find this institutional memory in municipal law in many states west of the Mississippi, so let me quote an article at length:

Before 1836 there were in Texas no incorporated cities in the modern meaning of the term. The Spanish municipality included not only the settlement itself, but also large areas of surrounding territory that might cover thousands of square miles. Under Mexican rule, these settlements continued to serve as nuclei of the units of local government. With the advent of the Republic of Texas, the Texas Congress began enacting laws incorporating cities in the state. City charters could only be granted by the legislature until adoption of a constitutional home-rule amendment in 1912. With the passage of the enabling act the following year, numerous cities with more than 5,000 in population began writing and adopting charters. These charters set forth the type of government under which the city would operate, established the number of individuals to serve on the governing body, and authorized the city to perform many of the functions required when large numbers of individuals chose to live in close proximity to one another. The state constitution provided that the city charters could authorize the individual city to govern itself, subject only to the constitution and general laws of the state...

The history of Texas municipalities as corporate entities began with the establishment of the Republic of Texas in 1836. Under Spanish and Mexican rule, municipality applied to not only a local settlement but also a broad area beyond. With the birth of the republic, the municipality became the county and the urban regions began to be incorporated, first by the [Republic of] Texas Congress and, after 1845, by the state legislature. The early congressional and special legislative acts were both articles of incorporation and charters; but all were specifically enacted by the central body. Home rule was not known.

However, the charter granted by the Texas Congress in 1837 to San Augustine, provided that the board of aldermen could pass any ordinance for the benefit of its inhabitants as long as it did not conflict with the laws or

---

[44] Everything west of the Mississippi except Oregon Territory, was claimed and ruled by Spain until 1800, when it gave the Louisiana Territory to France in trade for European and Caribbean lands. Thus, in 1800, Spain still ruled half of America!

constitution of the Republic of Texas. Similarly, in 1846 the legislature granted a special charter to New Braunfels, subject to ratification by the local voters at a special election. But the Texas Congress and later the state legislature, were very inconsistent. As late as 1911 – only a year before passage of the home-rule amendment – the City of Terrell was granted a special legislative charter in which its citizens were given no say, yet on the same day, March 20, the legislature enacted four other special legislative charters that were to become effective only upon ratification by the citizens of each community.

Through the last half of the nineteenth century and into the twentieth, the state continued to enact special legislative charters. Finally, in the early part of the twentieth century, the legislature realized that its time in Austin was being increasingly occupied by writing these charters. The growth of the cities in Texas was outstripping the legislature's ability to deal with local matters. The time to act had arrived. Other states had already granted home rule; Missouri was the first to do so, in 1875. Texas had struggled through an attempt to make special legislative charters work and had also tried to formulate general laws that would apply to both large and small cities. Neither effort was successful.

A constitutional amendment was passed in 1912 and followed in 1913 by the necessary enabling legislation. The amendment provides that any city with more than 5,000 population may by vote of its citizens adopt a home-rule charter. The charter may not contain any provision that is inconsistent with the state constitution or statutes, a restriction that still leaves these cities with more home rule than the cities of any other state in [America], according to a report by the Advisory Commission on Intergovernmental Relations, a federal research body.[45]

Zombie-Land Clown Show

When the servants go crazy, it's time for the People to do our chores. Donald Trump did the best he could by the lights he had. Some addled theorists were stridently claiming that Trump was still running the Republic from behind the scenes, with the help of the U.S. military, in a long-running secret operation. They hold this conspiracy theory: *"An illegal act of Congress in 1871 transformed our government into a corporation,*

---

[45] Terrell Blodgett, *Texas State Historical Association, Handbook of Texas* www.tshaonline.org/handbook I am proud of this project of my alma mater, the University of Texas; a fascinating compendium of American and Texas history.

made us all chattel property of the corporation, and all of us, our whole lives, have been the legal property of the Queen of England, the satanic Vatican and Freemasons, and certain banking families. But Trump will soon round them all up, and Trump's secret military operation will make everything right again! Just Trust the Plan!" Well, isn't that special?

Meanwhile, the People's two law enforcement institutions that we stipulate in the U.S. Constitution are idle because 'professional' lawyers have demonized the Grand Jury, and 'professional law enforcement' demonize the constitutional Militia. So, with no enforcement, the Constitution lies dormant and our Republic is increasingly a pathetic clown show, citizens clucking their tongues and shaking their fists online every day, yet doing none of the chores that We The People lay out for ourselves in the Constitution.

So we are living in a nightmare made possible by treacherous, complicit media – who Trump excoriated for years but then went right along with, by playing COVID Emperor to a fraud, with his boy Fauci and surrounding himself with Pharma executives. Sure, a nightmare run by usurpers in DC and tyrants in state palaces. But why do 80 million Trump supporters sit in the gulag doing nothing? We must all accept our share of blame. Lawlessness at the hands of all these 'professionals', are the wages of the People's own ignorance and apathy.

It is entirely up to the People in each county in America, to decide whether the 1-2 punch (COVID-19 Plandemic; Election Steal 2020) will go down in history as the most successful political dirty trick in history, or merely a target-rich environment for Grand Jury and Militia: the People's ultimate Home Rule against ruthless tyrants in state palaces, county elections boards, and corrupt police departments.

Arrogant, Lawless 'Professionals'

That lawful payback must *not* be executed by some lawless occupying military force, or by private 'militias', or by rioting in the streets, even if the criminal servants did it first.

Yes, it's true that for too long, too many in the so-called 'law enforcement' community have been committing tyrannical acts of thuggery fit for North Korea, just as Hitler's S.S. agents did. And for the same reason: their paychecks and benefits.

Every execrable 'professional' in a uniform who handcuffed mothers in playgrounds, business owners in their shops and homes, and Christians getting out of their cars to go to a worship service; and every 'law enforcement' thug who protected lawless legislators and ballot counters as they stole an election – should be indicted, tried, convicted, and sentenced to prison as a lesson to anyone who would "protect and serve" his career rather than his employers, the citizens.

And What's *Your* Excuse?

But enough about the armed agents of tyranny; *they do what they do because you will not do what you are <u>supposed</u> to do.*

Are *you* one of the millions of dumbfounded, ignorant Americans who allow your servants to throw the U.S. Constitution out the window, right along with the businesses of your neighbors, in exchange for illogical, medically preposterous 'safety' and a check from 'government' (your taxpaying neighbors)? Are you one who thinks that a stolen election has to just be put up with, "now that it's over with"?

Would you say that about criminals who make a clean getaway after a murder or robbery?

Or perhaps you were one of the millions who rallied, marched, and drove around with Trump flags out of your vehicle windows. What was that all about? Are you still in junior high, getting ready for the big Friday night game? Are rallies and posters and flags your idea of enforcing the Constitution and our rule of law?

And those who are still praying fervently that your savior will return in 2024, do you know anything at all about European history and Napoleon Buonaparte? If not, you should look it up.

Honestly, I give Trump the highest possible marks for effort; but his ego and lack of basic civics make him potentially as dangerous in the long term as the occupying usurpers in DC. But our bigger problem is the patriotic American who does not know basic civics and who does not *want* to know about his civic duty for Grand Jury and Militia service.

Incidentally, Militia entails many support functions that can be done from home by an 82-year-old woman as well as by a 22-year old man.

Repentance: A Responsible New Way of Life

Our servants at the state and federal levels are in high rebellion against the Constitution. This is the context in which we now act, *in extremis*. TACTICAL CIVICS™ is that tiny remnant of We The People who have the courage of their convictions, and who are willing to take responsibility beyond a few days' marches, or one parade or rally.

Let's be the grown-ups in the house, and put our collective foot down. This is no monarchy or imperial rule. There's no such thing as a 'law and order president', for goodness sakes; law and order are local matters, for every community to provide itself!

Whatever level of government rebels against the Constitution, We The People have authority and the duty to bring those servants back in line, through law enforcement. The institutions that We The People acknowledge in the Constitution for that purpose are the ancient law enforcement institutions, Grand Jury and Militia, as explained in this Volume 2, and in Volume 3 TACTICAL CIVICS™ Field Handbook.

Home Rule is consistent with the spirit and letter of the Declaration of Independence and the U.S. Constitution. Connecticut has the most historically unassailable Home Rule and Texas may have the most widespread Home Rule, but if you dig, you will find that Home Rule is consistent with your state's *original* Constitution. The problem is, We The People have slept for too long. When we gave up being statesmen ourselves and allowed careerist shysters to set their little cloven hoofs under the granite dome of our state palaces, we dug our own graves.

But we needn't lie in those open graves. No; the Vatican, Freemasons, and Queen of England do not own you, and our Republic is not, and never was, a corporation except perhaps in the minds of a few delusional elites and of conspiracy theorists who need to apply logic and common sense to the plain words of the U.S. Constitution.

We The People need to be more resourceful and determined than the criminals in our state palaces. Most Americans live in much worse states than mine; but too many of my fellow Texans applaud our rubber-sword, beady-eyed tyrant governor based on his self-serving sound bites instead of reviewing his actual (abysmal) record.

But we have a solution now. It's lawful, peaceful, practical, and can be perpetual. We can learn the lessons of history so as not to repeat them.

If you're ready to awake from this nightmare and get to work, we'll put you on the track and stay beside you every step, as you form your county chapter of TACTICAL CIVICS™ to finally give real teeth to our Constitution, restoring Home Rule in every town in our Republic.

Handbook Summary

Well, there you go. Grand Jury is no longer a mystery to you; but much more importantly, you see that this new way of life called TACTICAL CIVICS™ can only restore our civilization and our rule of law, and will only begin to arrest American corruption in school boards, city councils, county boards, state palaces, and the ultra-corrupt D.C. city-state, when We The People restore and serve on Grand Jury and Militia.

You now know how much *authority* you have always had. You know that when your chapter gets the Ordinance adopted, you can sign up to be on a roster to serve on the next Grand Jury, and that you and your fellow citizens can confidentially report possible felony crimes on the new Grand Jury web page for your county government.

Grand Juries must be impaneled whenever an obvious crime has been committed in your county and must be addressed by a criminal court. As I write this, we still do not know how justice will be restored against the obvious theft of the 2020 election and seating of countless people who were illegally seated in office at all levels. This is the most serious constitutional crisis in the history of our Republic.

Will a civil war ensue if the Communists refuse to give in, and refuse to have Trump take his rightful office and begin reversing all the lawless, insane, un-American things that resident Biden has done? If civil war arises, which side will the federal troops be on? Today, it appears a toss-up; as many seem to be willing to trample and violate the Constitution and America's godly heritage, as those who will defend them. Only God knows. For our part, we believe that the only way that God will cease His judgment is our sincere repentance and a return to our duties.

That is the mission of AmericaAgain! Trust, and its action mission TACTICAL CIVICS™, the initial planning for which began 13 years ago when Bush II was in office, continuing the globalist destruction that the Clintons had begun. Missions of this magnitude take time.

But now you realize that once you're serving on the Grand Jury, you and your fellow panel members really do run the show. You can decide whether to even allow the prosecutor to be in your chambers while you deliberate. You can task the sheriff and staff to execute your summonses and warrants for evidence. If the sheriff is under suspicion or possibly in cahoots with the target, you can call on your County Militia to do the job. As we have explained (and you can learn much more in Volume 3 of this Field Handbook), a well-trained County Militia is as vital to our future as is an educated County Grand Jury.

You have learned that our Common Law is over a thousand years old; that our Constitution established the most powerful system of self-government in history; and that our 'supreme Law of the Land' depends entirely on the People being active, educated Militia and Grand Jury.

You now see what a clever distraction politics is, and after so many years of corruption in every level of government, politics can never substitute for law enforcement. The 'Deep Axis' in this war consists of the globalist cabal whose god is money. It includes all major media, Big Tech, Hollywood, K-12 government schools, most universities, multinational corporations, major retailers, and most sports teams. The Deep Axis is proudly opposed to Christianity, common sense, and rule of law. They incite riots, racial division, cultural breakdown, and an increasing avalanche of official corruption in federal 'alphabet' agencies and the military.

Thus, ours is a pivotal time in American history. With the onslaught of atheists, growing ranks of sexual perverts, baby-murderers, and racial strife-mongers, our civilization is doomed unless We The People in the vast, conservative American heartland repent before God and act courageously and diligently to restore our rule of law. Then the People of God can defeat the 150-year-long march of American Communism!

In the coming years, after repenting before God, there is no more important service you can render your Republic than to start or join your county TACTICAL CIVICS™ chapter, help get our County Grand Jury Ordinance passed and a Grand Jury section added to your county government's website, and volunteer for Grand Jury duty.

When you do, now you can educate your entire Grand Jury Panel and have them download this handbook in free PDF at TacticalCivics.com

Repentance is an action word.

APPENDIX A
Scalia, U.S. v. Williams (1992)

This is a reprint of only the germane portions of Part III of Antonin Scalia's ruling for the majority in the U.S. supreme Court's case U.S. v. Williams (1992). In this excerpt for potential Grand Jurors, we have also removed Scalia's lengthy case cites and their quotation marks that interrupt the flow of ideas for non-lawyers. We also *emphasized with italics* the key takeaways of Scalia's constitutional law lesson in the Williams ruling. For the full text of the majority opinion and dissent... https://www.law.cornell.edu/supct/html/90-1972.ZO.html

~~~

Because *the Grand Jury is an institution separate from the courts, over whose functioning the courts do not preside*, we think it clear that, as a general matter at least, no such supervisory judicial authority exists...

Rooted in long centuries of Anglo-American history, the Grand Jury is mentioned in the Bill of Rights, but not in the body of the Constitution. It has not been textually assigned, therefore, to any of the branches described in the first three Articles. *It is a constitutional fixture in its own right.*

The theory of its function is that it belongs to no branch of the institutional government, serving as a kind of buffer or referee between the government and the People. Although the Grand Jury normally operates, of course, in the courthouse and under judicial auspices, its institutional relationship with the judicial branch has traditionally been, so to speak, at arm's length. [The] *judges' direct involvement in the functioning of the Grand Jury has generally been confined to the constitutive one of calling the Grand Jurors together and administering their oaths of office.*

The Grand Jury's functional independence from the judicial branch is evident both in the scope of its power to investigate criminal wrongdoing, and in the manner in which that power is exercised. Unlike a court, whose jurisdiction is predicated upon a specific case or controversy, the *Grand Jury can investigate merely on suspicion that the law is being violated, or even because it wants assurance that it is not. It need not identify the offender it suspects, or even the precise nature of the offense it is investigating. The Grand Jury requires no authorization from its constituting court to initiate an investigation, nor does the prosecutor require leave of court to seek a Grand Jury indictment.*

In its day-to-day functioning, the Grand Jury generally operates without the interference of a presiding judge. It swears in its own witnesses and deliberates in total secrecy…Even in this setting, however, *we have insisted that the Grand Jury remain free to pursue its investigations unhindered by external influence or supervision…*

Recognizing this tradition of independence, we have said that the Fifth Amendment's constitutional guarantee presupposes an investigative body acting *independently of either prosecuting attorney or judge…*

No doubt in view of the Grand Jury proceeding's status as other than a constituent element of a criminal prosecution (U.S. Const., Amdt. VI), we have said that certain constitutional protections afforded defendants in criminal proceedings have no application before that body. *The Double Jeopardy Clause of the Fifth Amendment does not bar a Grand Jury from returning an indictment when a prior Grand Jury has refused to do so.* We have twice suggested…that *the Sixth Amendment right to counsel does not attach when an individual is summoned to appear before a Grand Jury, even if he is the subject of the investigation.*

And although the Grand Jury may not force a witness to answer questions in violation of the Fifth Amendment's constitutional guarantee against self-incrimination, our cases suggest that *an indictment obtained through the use of evidence previously obtained in violation of the privilege against self-incrimination is nevertheless valid.*

Given the Grand Jury's operational separateness from its constituting court, it should come as no surprise that we have been reluctant to invoke the judicial supervisory power as a basis for prescribing modes of Grand Jury procedure. Over the years, we have received many requests to exercise supervision over the Grand Jury's evidence-taking process, but we have refused them all...because of the potential injury to *the historic role and functions of the Grand Jury.* In Costello v. United States, we declined to enforce the hearsay rule in Grand Jury proceedings, since that would run counter to *the whole history of the Grand Jury institution, in which laymen conduct their inquiries unfettered by technical rules...*

It is axiomatic that the Grand Jury sits not to determine guilt or innocence, but to assess whether there is adequate basis for bringing a criminal charge...and to make the assessment, it has always been thought sufficient to hear only the prosecutor's side. As Blackstone described the prevailing practice in 18th-century England, the Grand Jury was only to hear evidence on behalf of the prosecution, for the finding of an indictment is only in the nature of an enquiry or accusation, which is afterwards to be tried and determined. *[N]either in this country nor in England has the suspect under investigation by the Grand Jury ever been thought to have a right to testify, or to have exculpatory evidence presented...*

We accepted Justice Nelson's description in Costello v. United States, where we held that it would run counter to the whole history of the Grand Jury institution to permit an indictment to be challenged on the ground that there was incompetent or inadequate evidence before the Grand Jury...

APPENDIX B
County Ordinance on Grand Jury

An **ORDINANCE** Providing for Citizens to Volunteer for Grand
Jury and Assuring   that the County Court shall
Call for a Grand Jury When the People so Demand,
in the County/Municipality

of_____,

in the State of_____

Short Title: County Ordinance on Grand Jury

Preamble

We, the [name of county board or commission] *of* [fill in] [COUNTY,
PARISH OR BOROUGH], [fill in STATE], *in pursuance of our oaths to
uphold the Constitutions of our State and of the United States, and of our duty
to our community under Divine Law, hereby secure the fundamental right and
authority of our Citizens to volunteer for Grand Jury service within this* [County,
Parish or Borough].

Article I. Justification

*§1 WHEREAS, in the preamble to the Constitution for the United States, the
American People declare that, "We The People…do ordain and establish this
Constitution", thus clearly establishing that The People collectively occupy the
highest sovereignty over all American government; and*

*§2 WHEREAS, the United States supreme Court in Chisolm v. Georgia, U.S.
2 Dall 419, 454 (1793), affirmed that, "The People are Sovereign…at the
Revolution, the sovereignty devolved on the people; and they are truly the sovereigns
of the country…equal as fellow citizens, and as joint tenants in the sovereignty";
and*

*§3 WHEREAS, in Amendment X of the U.S. Constitution, we state, pari
materia with the Preamble, that We The People, as well as the State governments*

that We elect to represent us, retain all powers not specifically enumerated by us in the U.S. Constitution; and

§4 WHEREAS, the Grand Jury, along with the Militia, are the two ancient and pre-constitutional institutions intended and stipulated by the U.S. Constitution to maintain our rule of law and to 'execute' that and all other laws in our Republic; and

§5 WHEREAS, if our State enacts any statute that violates or is repugnant to the U.S. Constitution, that State law is null and void ab initio; and

§6 WHEREAS, no State legislature can sideline or outlaw the Grand Jury institution or impair its functionality, as it remains an independent institution of the People, pre-dating the U.S. Constitution but demanded thereby; and

§7 WHEREAS, Rule 6(a)(1) of the Federal Rules of Criminal Procedure stipulates, "When the public interest so requires, the court must order that one or more grand juries be summoned."; and

§8 WHEREAS, in times of corruption and lack of public confidence, the public must be the sole determinant of its own interest rather than public employees deciding what is the public interest; and

§9 WHEREAS, different county and state governments observe a variety of protocols allowing or disallowing the citizens to place their names on a volunteer roster for Grand Jury service;

Article II. Ordered

§1 NOW, THEREFORE, BE IT RESOLVED, that the [Board, Commission,] *of* _____ [County, Parish or Borough] *hereby orders that within this jurisdiction, any citizen and resident who has not been convicted of a felony and who applies to be placed on a standby roster for Grand Jury duty, shall be placed on that roster by the county clerk; and*

§2 For any given occasion requiring seating of a Grand Jury, all names on the volunteer standby roster shall be added to any other list used as a source of names for random jury selection, and from this aggregated list Grand Jurors shall be selected truly at random, in no particular order nor assigned to any particular case or Grand Jury target; and

§3 Each random selection session of Grand Jurors by county clerk staff shall be witnessed in person by a three-member committee of this governing body to assure

that the process is uncorrupted by any staffer or potential Grand Jury target or the target's minions, contractors, or associates; and

§4 If any judge in our jurisdiction shall refuse to call for a Grand Jury venire when demanded by petition signed by a number of County residents equal to or greater than half of one percent of the number of ballots cast in the prior county election, this representative body shall seek from the State Court of Appeals or Supreme Court a writ of mandamus compelling drawing of a venire, or the appointment of an alternate judge to call for such Grand Jury to grant relief to the community; and

§5 The County shall make a page or pages available on its web site or prominently post links there, for County Grand Jury education, information, volunteer application with the County Clerk, and for Citizens to submit legitimate complaints of possible crimes, and calls for a Grand Jury if a panel is not sitting at that time.

Article III. Miscellaneous Provisions

§1 SEVERABILITY. If any section, part or provision of this Ordinance is declared unconstitutional or invalid by a court of competent jurisdiction, then it is expressly provided and it is the intention of the [name of county board or commission] in passing this Ordinance that its parts shall be severable and all other parts of this Ordinance shall not be affected thereby and they shall remain in full force and effect.

§2 EFFECTIVE DATE. This Ordinance shall take effect immediately upon its passage.

ORDAINED *by the* [name of county board or commission] *of* [fill in] [COUNTY, PARISH OR BOROUGH], [fill in STATE], *this* _____*Day of* [month] *in the Year of our Lord 20____*

_____

[Board/Commission Member]

_____

[Board/Commission Member]

_____

[Board/Commission Member]

_____

[Board/Commission Member]

_____

[Board/Commission Member]

MODCOGJORDrev04

APPENDIX C
Jury Panel Size & Officers, by State

The size of state Grand Juries varies widely. If a state convenes Grand Juries that range in size (e.g., 12 to 18 jurors) we show '12-18 jurors'. If a state uses a different number of jurors for different *kinds* of Grand Juries, the list indicates this by noting that the size can be '23 or 11 or 19' jurors. Next to each state abbreviation is a citation of the court rule, statute, or case that sets the size. (Source: Susan Brenner & Lori Shaw)

State and Source of Information	No. Jurors (Quorum)
AL: CRIMINAL PROCEDURE RULE 12.2(a)	18 (13)
AK: CRIMINAL PROCEDURE RULE 6(d)	12-18 (12)
AZ: REVISED STATUTES '21-322(B)	12-16 (9)
AR: CODE '16-32-201(c)	16 (12)
CA: PENAL CODE "888 & 88.2	23 or 11 or 19 (4 or 8 or 12)
CO: REVISED STATUTES '13-72-102	12 or 23 (9)
CT: GENERAL STATUTES '54-47(b)(3)	1-3 (n/a)
DE: CODE tit. 10 '4505	10 or 15 (9 or 7)
FL: STATUTES "905.01(1) & 905.37(3)	15-18 (12 or 15)
GA: CODE '15-12-61(a) & '15-12-100(b)	16-23 (16)
HI: CRIMINAL PROCEDURE RULE 6(a)	16 (8)
ID: CODE "2-103 & 2-502	16 (12)
IL: REVISED STATUTES ch. 705 &305/16	16 (12)
IN: CODE '35-34-2-2(a)	6 (5)
IA: CRIMINAL PROCEDURE RULE 3(1)	7 (5)

KS: STATUTES '22-3001(3)	15 (12)
KY: REVISED STATUTES '29A.200	12 (9)
LA: CRIMNAL PROCEDURE CODE 413A	12 (9)
ME: CRIMINAL PROCEDURE RULE 6(a)	13-23 (13)
MD: Atty Grv Comm v Bailey, 285 Md. 631, 403 A.2d 1261	23 (12)
MA: GENERAL LAWS ch. 277 '2	23 (12)
MI: COMPILED LAWS '767.11	13-17 (13)
MN: STATUTES '628.41(1)	16-23 (16)
MS: CODE '13-5-41	15-20 (15)
MO: CONSTITUTION art. I '16	12 (12)
MT: CODE 3-15-103	11 (11)
NE: STATUTES '25-1633	16 (12)
NV: REVISED STATUTES "6.110 & 6.120	17 (12)
NH: State v. Fleury, 114 N.H. 325, 321 A.2d 108 (N.H. 1974)	23 (12)
NJ: STATUTES '2A:73-1	23 (12)
NM: STATUTES '31-6-1	12 (12)
NY: CRIMINAL PROCEDURE LAW '190.05	16-23 (16)
NC: GENERAL STATUTES '15A-621	12-18 (12)
ND: CODE "29-10.1-01; 29-10.2-03	8-11 (8)
OH: CRIMINAL PROCEDURE RULE 6(A)	9 (9)
OK: STATUTES tit. 22 '311	12 (12)
OR: REVISED STATUTES '132.010	7 (5)
PA: CRIMINAL PROCEDURE RULE 253(a)	23 (15)
RI: GENERAL LAWS "12-11-1 & 12-11.1-1	13-23 (12-23)
SC: CODE "14-7-1510 & 14-7-1620	18 (12)
SD: CODIFIED LAWS '23A-5-1	6-10 (6)
TN: CODE '40-12-206(a)	13 (12)

TX: CONSTITUTION art. v '13	12 (9)
UT: CODE '77-10a-4(1)	9-15 (9)
VT: CRIMINAL PROCEDURE RULE 6(a)	18-23 (18)
VA: CODE '19.2-195	5 or 7 (5 or 7)
WA: REVISED CODE '10.27.020(6)	12 (12)
WV: CRIMINAL PROCEDURE RULE 6(a)	16 (15)
WI: STATUTES '756.10(5)	17 (14)
WY: STATUTES '7-5-103(a)	12 (9)

Grand Jury Officers

County Grand Juries have a foreman, who administers the oath to witnesses testifying before the grand jury, sees that it receives other kinds of evidence, and generally runs the Grand Jury's sessions.

Forty-nine states (all except CT) retain the office of Grand Jury foreman, but three states – Idaho, Kansas and Wyoming--use the term 'presiding juror' rather than foreman. Connecticut does not need the grand jury foreperson because it eliminated Grand Jury composed of citizens and created a bogus 'grand jury' composed of a judge!

Of the 49 states that have a foreperson/presiding juror, 24 give this officer a deputy. Five states add another officer: In Florida, North Dakota, Oregon and South Dakota, this person is known as the grand jury's clerk; in Nevada (s)he is the grand jury's secretary.

F – have a foreman   **DF** – also have a deputy foreman
PJ – have a 'presiding juror' instead   **DPJ** – also have a 'deputy presiding juror'   **CL** – have a clerk   **SY** – have a secretary

Next to each state abbreviation is a citation of the court rule, statute, or case that creates the Grand Jury officer positions.
(Source: Susan Brenner & Lori Shaw)

State and Source of Information	Officers
AL: CRIMINAL PROCEDURE RULE 12.5(a)	F & DF
AK: CRIMINAL PROCEDURE RULE 6(h)	F & DF
AZ: RULES OF CRIMINAL PROCEDURE 12.4(a)	F & DF
AR: CODE § 16-85-501(a)-(b)	F & CL
CA: PENAL CODE §§ 912 & 916.1	F & DF
CO: REVISED STATUTES ANNOTATED § 13-72-104	F & DF
CT: GENERAL STATUTES ANNOTATED § 54-47(b)(3)	Not Applicable
DE: SUPERIOR COURT CRIMINAL RULES 6(c)	F & DF
FL: STATUTES ANNOTATED §§ 905.08 & 905.13	F, DF & CL
GA: CODE ANNOTATED §§ 15-12-67(a) & 15-12-100(b)	F
HI: RULES OF PENAL PROCEDURE 6(c)	F & DF
ID: RULES OF CRIMINAL PROCEDURE 6(a)	PJ & DPJ
IL: REVISED STATUTES ch. 705 & 305/17	F
IN: CODE ANNOTATED § 35-34-2-3(d)	F & CL
IA: RULES OF CRIMINAL PROCEDURE 3(4)(a)	F
KS: STATUTES ANNOTATED § 22-3004	PJ & DPJ
KY: REVISED STAT ANN § 29a.250 & RULES CRIM PROC § 5.04	F
LA: CODE CRIMNAL PROCEDURE ANNOTATED 413(b)-(c)	F
ME: RULES OF CRIMINAL PROCEDURE 6(c)	F & DF
MD: CODE ANNOTATED, CTS. & JUD. PROCEDURE § 9-118(b)	F
MA: RULES OF CRIMINAL PROCEDURE 5(b)	F
MI: COMPILED LAWS ANNOTATED §§ 767.11 & 767.12	F
MN: STATUTES §§ 628.56& 628.57	F & CL
MS: CODE ANN § 13-5-45 & UNIF RULES CIR. & CTY. CT. 7.02	F
MO: ANNOTATED STATUTES § 540.090	F

MT: CODE ANNOTATED 46-11-303	F
NE: REVISED STATUTES § 29-1403	F
NV: REVISED STATUTES § 172.075	F, DF & SY
NH: REVISED STATUTES ANNOTATED §§ 600:4 & 600:5	F & CL
NJ: RULES OF CRIM PROC 3:6-4 & STAT ANN § 2a:73-3	F & DF
NM: STATUTES ANNOTATED § 31-6-2	F
NY: CRIMINAL PROCEDURE LAW § 190.20(3) (McKinney 1995)	F, DF & SY
NC: GENERAL STATUTES § 15a-622	F
ND: CENT. CODE §§ 29-10.1-11 & 29-10.1-15	F, DF & CL
OH: RULES OF CRIM PROC 6(c) & REV CODE ANN § 2939.02	F
OK: STATUTES ANNOTATED tit. 22 §§ 323 & 328	F & CL
OR: REVISED STATUTES §§ 132.050 & 132.080	F, DF & CL
PA: RULES OF CRIM PROC 253(g) & CONS. STAT ANN § 4545(c)	F & SY
RI: SUPERIOR RULES OF CRIMINAL PROCEDURE 6(a)	F & DF
SC: CODE ANNOTATED §§ 14-7-1580 & 14-7-1670	F & DF
SD: CODIFIED LAWS § 23a-5-6	F, DF & CL
TN: RULES OF CRIMINAL PROCEDURE 6(g)	F
TX: CRIMINAL PROCEDURE CODE ART. 19.34	F
UT: CODE ANNOTATED § 77-10a-11(1)	F & DF
VT: RULES OF CRIMINAL PROCEDURE 6(c)	F & DF
VA: CODE ANNOTATED §§ 19.2-197 & 19.2.207	F
WA: REVISED CODE ANNOTATED § 10.27.070(1)	F & DF
WV: RULES OF CRIMINAL PROCEDURE RULE 6(c)	F & DF
WI: STATUTES ANNOTATED § 756.12	F & CL
WY: RULES OF CRIMINAL PROCEDURE 6(a)(7)(a)	PJ & DPJ

101

APPENDIX D
Further Reading

If the history of our Constitution and legal system interest you, or if you'd like homeschool resources to allow your older child to leapfrog their cohorts in pre-law programs – or just want to draw your fellow Grand Jurors into interesting discussions beyond today's silly news, try these works. I promise you'll never be the same.

~~~

The Supremacists: The Tyranny of Judges & How to Stop It (Phyllis Schlafly) The late Phyllis Schlafly had a far greater legal mind than Sandra Day O'Connor. In this little hardback, she expounds on what TACTICAL CIVICS™ put into our Reform Law #2, the Constitutional Courts Act.

Is Administrative Law Unlawful? (Philip Hamburger; Professor of Law, Columbia) How did real judges allow an entire fake 'court' racket to build a European-style bureaucratic cancer of 'administrative law' that isn't actual law at all? Professor Hamburger grinds it all out.

The Problem With Lincoln by Thomas J. DiLorenzo debunks the legends offered as reasons for Lincoln's war. The author exposes why Lincoln suspended *habeas corpus,* why he imprisoned thousands of Northern war dissenters, and why he shut down hundreds of opposition newspapers. The author also exposes Lincoln's real economic agenda. If you wonder why you weren't taught this in school, start realizing that the rich really, truly love their riches and are as ruthless as they are treacherous, smiles and all.

Lincoln's Marxists: Marxism in the Civil War by Walter D. Kennedy and Al Benson, Jr. is another of those books that convinced me that I was cheated even in my expensive private education. The book exposes Union army generals that were Marxists, and the Marxist ideas that informed the Lincoln administration. I voted GOP for 25 years because I thought the GOP was the party that would conserve the Constitution. How little I knew about the history of the GOP's founding and its Red Roots! Rather than the party of individual liberty, it has always been the power center for American mercantilists and bankers.

The TACTICAL CIVICS Ready Constitution is a spiral-bound, super-handy desk copy of the U.S. Constitution with a unique design. It features Mike Holler's numbering system for each clause in the Constitution, making it easy to start memorizing where your favorite clauses are. Amendments are integrated in context where they affect the law. Buy this handy edition in the Training Center. I use it every day.

Free, Sovereign, and Independent States: The Intended Meaning of the American Constitution by John Remington Graham explains the U.S. Constitution clause by clause, tracing legislative history from the kings' courts and parliaments of Great Britain to our Constitutional Convention. This ready reference on every clause in the Constitution is a masterful briefing on the origins of America's Supreme Law. Bottom line: this is the concise, historically complete explanation of every sentence in the U.S. Constitution.

The Founders' Constitution by editors Kurland and Lerner is a 5-volume massive reference set offering a more in-depth treatment than Graham's. It includes extracts from leading works of political theory, history, law, and constitutional argument that the Framers and their contemporaries used and produced. Available in paperback and CD-ROM, I find the electronic edition considerably handier. Bottom line: this is a far more in-depth background on the U.S. Constitution than Graham's book above, but Graham's work is more comprehensive regarding the provenance (legal roots) of every clause.

The People Themselves: Popular Constitutionalism and Judicial Review by Larry D. Kramer, former dean of Stanford Law School, is no dry tome filled with legal jargon. It is a refreshing look at why We The People have more lawful power than the U.S. Supreme Court. Dean Kramer discusses why it is critical that We The People begin to exercise that power peacefully and lawfully – or we will lose that power, and rule of law with it. Unfortunately, Dr. Kramer is now the president of a large, very liberal Silicon Valley foundation, but his thesis in this work still holds true. Bottom line: We the People have more power and authority than any U.S. supreme Court; we just don't take advantage of it. Until now!

104

The First American Republic 1774-1789 by Thomas Chorlton is similar to an out of print book called _President Who?: Forgotten Founders_ by Stanley Klos. George Washington called Payton Randolph "the Father of our country" because Randolph was the first President of the United States in Congress Assembled, and 14 presidential administrations existed prior to that of George Washington! Read this one and you'll agree that most of us were cheated in our education.

The Republic of Letters: The Correspondence Between Jefferson and Madison 1776-1826 a 3-volume compendium of 50 years' correspondence between the two giants among America's founding fathers. Series editor James Smith makes segues from their correspondence to their historical context, helping the reader grasp these founders' development over their lifetimes. I learned more about Madison from these letters than from seven Madison biographies. To grasp a man's mind, read his letters.

Democracy in America by Alexis deTocqueville is a classic work of economics, sociology, and political science. Although the young Frenchman did not grasp the republican form of government guaranteed in our Constitution, he was prescient about _democracy_ in America. Our founders created a representative constitutional republic of sovereign States specifically to _avoid_ democracy, majority rule that always degenerates into warring mobs, grabbing for goodies from the all-knowing Nanny State.

From his limited view as a foreigner, Tocqueville accurately predicted that democracy in America would degenerate into soft despotism and tyranny of the majority as Madison predicted 50 years earlier.

Tocqueville said that majoritarian tyranny would spring from the confluence of two corrupting factors: dependence on government for material security, and the growing prejudices of an increasingly ignorant mass, against one another's factions and groups. He was correct. After 150 years of government education, most Americans are European socialists, unfit to rule our passions and unwilling to oversee our servant government; instead, making it their master by begging security and provision from it.

A Tax Honesty Primer is my little booklet and TaxHonestyPrimer.com website. Having read the Internal Revenue Code, countless court rulings and cases, seven books on Tax Honesty, and dozens of websites over two years, I then became a law-abiding Nontaxpayer 27 years ago. I couldn't find in one place enough information to take action and expose the corruption, so I created *A Tax Honesty Primer* as the first step in Taxpayer due diligence, so that others can avoid years of wading through tax protester theories. The book is not my opinion or 'position'; it's a compendium of easily verifiable facts, court rulings, Tax Code sections, federal regulations, jury verdicts, former IRS commissioner and IRS employee statements, and well-settled law. On the site, I do not sell anything or accept donations.

Tax Honesty is wonderful defense for the self-employed (it's all but impossible if you work for someone else, especially a large company); but playing defense will never arrest Congress' crimes. Until our Indictment Engine™ becomes our permanent citizen mechanism to arrest organized crime in Congress, at least Tax Honesty offers short-term relief. Like 'household secession' from Congress' corruption.

The Official Counterfeiter is a 36-page free cartoon booklet created in 1969 by Vic Lockman; the clearest explanation I've ever read, of Congress' money and banking crimes on behalf of the corrupt banking industry. The link to the booklet is:

http://scripturalscrutinydotcom.files.wordpress.com/2012/01/the-official-counterfeiter-biblical-economics.pdf

The American Deep State is Peter Dale Scott's best book yet, of over 40 books published over 42 years, exposing the Deep State. The author has spent his adult life laying a trail of primary-source evidence for the shocking and revealing assertions in his books. The Deep State refers to the banking, war, and oil industries together with the 'intelligence' industry in all its secret agencies. Every foreign war the USA has fought has been instigated by, and directly benefited the Deep State. This shadow government is un-elected, unaccountable, invisible to productive Americans, and ruthless. It first sought to hijack the Constitution through Hamilton and Clay, finally succeeding with Lincoln and ever since. *If you read only one book on the list, make it this one.*

The Sovereign Individual by James Davidson & Lord William Rees-Mogg explains the shake-up of nations introduced by the Internet, much like the impact that the movable-type printing press had in medieval times. Even now, 18 years after the first edition of this book, the world's institutions have not come to grips with the Internet. But the news is daily illustrating the acceleration of revolution against wicked and bloated industries, institutions, and governments. As institutions attempt to deal with newly-liberated humanity, the authors posit that informed individuals and small businesses will win, and big governments and institutions will lose. AmericaAgain! agrees with this assessment.

Hamilton's Curse: How Jefferson's Arch Enemy Betrayed the American Revolution – and What it Means for Americans Today by Thomas J. DiLorenzo (2009) is a long-overdue correction of the record about Alexander Hamilton. Although a courageous hero of our War for Independence, Hamilton was a wily tactician in laying the foundation for America's corrupt banking industry, and perhaps the most destructive 'founding father'. DiLorenzo debunks the long-held legends that deify Hamilton, exposing the man for what he was: a conniving, self-absorbed con artist. In the final chapter, *Ending the Curse,* I find nothing upon which to disagree with the author except that, like most authors offering reform proposals, he fails to offer a mechanism to *enact* his solutions.

Against Our Better Judgment by Alison Weir is only 93 pages of body text, followed by 107 pages of endnotes. With most professional academics being paid shills of the Deep State and its private foundations, a reader should not look for truth and authors' credentials to jibe. This book is copiously documented, with almost 375 references. Does Israel control Washington DC? Read, and decide.

JFK-9/11: 50 Years of the Deep State I disagree with his dismissal of Old Testament Scripture, but Frenchman Laurent Guyenot is a Renaissance man with degrees in engineering and Medieval Studies who worked in the arms industry and also authored a study on the psychological and social damage of mass pornography. In this book, Guyenot offers an even better analysis of 9/11 than Ruppert's book, in that he demonstrates the Deep State sponsorship of both the JFK assassination and the 9/11 attacks. Bottom line: the smoking gun of both Deep State actions leads to the Israeli Mossad and the CIA.

The Fourth Turning: What the Cycles of History Tell Us About America's Next Rendezvous With Destiny by William Strauss and Neil Howe is a smaller, more exciting 1998 follow-up to their 1991 book *Generations: The History of America's Future.* In this national bestseller, Strauss and Howe illustrate the historical 80- to 100-year cycle called a *saecula,* further divided into five 20-year periods/generations. The authors call each transition between these generations, a *turning*. Thus in 1998, the authors accurately predicted the fourth turning of our *saecula;* a crisis period from 2005-2015. This was fulfilled in the Ron Paul Revolution, TEA Party movement, 'Great Recession', collapse of the U.S. Dollar, and increasing mistrust of institutions. Tracing 'heroic' generations back to pre-colonial times, the authors conclude that by 2015, Americans in the 'Baby Boomer' and 'Thirteener' generations would step up to meet the crisis, and we are. (Chicken Little is dead wrong.)

Consent of the Governed (Jason W. Hoyt) A Grand Jury primer that goes into much more detail than the booklet in your hand. While Jason has too much 'marketing style' and tries to paint Grand Jury alone as the solution, we still highly recommend his book.

The People's Panel (Richard D. Younger) is out of print but available as a PDF loaner online, and TACTICAL CIVICS™ will soon offer a paperback reprint. The history of how the bureaucrats and legal industry tried to kill off Grand Jury in America as they did in England.

Excellence of the Common Law, Compared and Contrasted With Civil Law in Light of History, Nature, and Scripture (Brent Allan Winters; self-published, 2008) Ever wondered how our sophisticated and complex system of law evolved from Neolithic, nomadic tribes clubbing one another over the head in the British isles, Scandinavia and ancient Goth lands? Or how our legal system was drawn from Scripture? This 957-page masterpiece is the best work explaining the history and design of our legal system, and its roots in Scripture.

The History of English Law before the Time of Edward I (Sir Frederick Pollock & Frederic William Maitland) The two-volume classic of western legal history. A colorful, detailed survey.

A Concise History of the Common Law (Theodore F.T. Plucknett) A good history of our Common Law system if you lack the time for Brent Winters' big tome, or Pollock and Maitland's.

Government by Judiciary: The Transformation of the Fourteenth Amendment (Raoul Berger; Senior Fellow in American Legal History, Harvard) We often write about "Lincoln's hijacking of America"; Congress first counterfeiting real money with worthless paper, ending State Militias with full-time 'U.S. Army' violating our Constitution, then passing the 14th Amendment. Professor Berger exposes that last crime.

About the Author

David M. Zuniga is a graduate of the University of Texas (BS, Architectural Engineering) and was for 28 years a professional engineer designing schools, churches, industrial and commercial buildings. He has been a cattleman, custom homebuilder, commercial contractor, SCUBA instructor, missionary pilot, and land surveyor.

Having founded four classical Christian K-12 schools in three states, he designed a curriculum with Latin, Logic, Rhetoric, and the Great Books of Western Civilization.

Shocked at the government fraud of 9/11, beginning in 2006 he spent 14 months in monastic seclusion, prayer and study of 110 key books. He wrote the first draft of the AmericaAgain! Declaration and refined the document with the help of many fine Americans including constitutionalist radio show host Mike Church and constitutional scholar and author Edwin Vieira Jr.

Establishing AmericaAgain! Trust with his brother in 2009, David wrote his first book *This Bloodless Liberty* in 2010 to convey his vision. In 2015 he published *Fear The People,* introducing a full-spectrum action plan to restore popular sovereignty and rule of law. In 2018, he began writing the 5-volume Tactical Civics™ series to break down this new way of life into brief books for action. With his co-founders, in January 2021 David helped launch the TACTICAL CIVICS™ Training Center and by June, Americans had launched over 160 county chapters.

David has been a guest on Infowars Nightly News and is a recurring guest on radio shows across the republic. His published articles have appeared on many blogs, forums and alternative media.

David has two children and six grandchildren. They live in the Hill Country of Texas where they serve no king but King Jesus.

Made in the USA
Monee, IL
07 January 2022

88321546R00066